SkateTalk

SkateTalk

FIGURE SKATING IN THE WORDS OF THE STARS

Steve Milton

FIREFLY BOOKS

*storytellers; and to the warm
quietly urging me on*

A FIREFLY BOOK

Cataloguing in Publication Data

Milton, Steve
      Skatetalk : figure skating in the words of the stars

ISBN 1-55209-209-7

1. Skating – History. 2. Skating. I. Title.

GV850.4.M545   1998   796.91'2'09   C97-932378-9

Published in the United States in 1998
by Firefly Books (U.S.) Inc.
P.O. Box 1338
Ellicot Station
Buffalo, New York, USA
14205

Design: Jean Lightfoot Peters
Electronic formatting: Frank Zsigo

Printed and bound in Canada

98 99 00 01 6 5 4 3 2 1

CONTENTS

9. THE STORYTELLERS 205

PREFACE

Figure skating speaks to us in so many languages.

I don't mean this as much in the literal sense—that there were 44 countries entered in the International Skating Union World Championships, representing nearly that many native tongues and dialects—as in the figurative.

A dozen people can watch the same skating event and come away with a dozen different, indelible impressions. And when a distinct, definable impression has been cast upon you, then you have been communicated with. And that is the very heart of language.

Skating speaks to our physical side. We can appreciate, even without grasping the technicalities, the sheer power and athletic supremacy of a quadruple jump in combination with a triple jump. Seven revolutions in less than two seconds, catapulting from an impossibly narrow piece of steel and returning to it. Creating so much torque that a loss of control at the wrong moment can shred knee ligaments.

Skating converses freely with the aesthetic living in all of us. Lucinda Ruh eases into one of her tulip-on-a-turntable spins, and something warm and familiar percolates within us. We forget that she is in 16th place, that her jumps are not up to those of the other women. We instantly recognize those liquid revolutions: they are what we know as "beautiful."

Skating splashes about in our emotional reservoir. Against all odds and in his hometown, Rudy Galindo wins the U.S. Championship, bearing scars of heartbreak so fresh they could burst open again at any time. And we collapse under the overwhelming sentiment of the moment. Favorite skaters fall several times, finish their programs in tears, and we are flushed with empathy. Torvill and Dean with their interpretation of *Bolero* stir our passion; Philippe Candeloro triggers our laughter; the expressive Toller Cranston and the fragile Ekaterina Gordeeva cause us to weep; Elvis Stojko gives us pause with his determined fierceness.

Skating talks right out loud to our competitive nature. It is a sport as well as an art form. The relief that Ina and Dungjen felt on finally winning; the joy that was Tara Lipinski's following her triumph at the World Championships; the recovery Michelle Kwan made after losing the U.S. Championship; the defeat that Underhill and Martini faced and overcame in 1984; the pain that Brian Orser endured for so long after the 1988 Olympics—these highs and lows are constant to all sport. Wherever there is winning and losing, they will flourish.

Skating speaks, increasingly, the hip jargon of youth, the universal language of music, the demanding howl of money, the many tongues of politics, even the sobering moan of death.

And skating speaks through the voices of its people. Those voices are what this book is about. Through the testimony of the dozens of athletes, coaches and administrators who have volunteered their time to speak with me, I've gained new insights into their character and their sport. I hope this book can help you gain them, too. Although the skating world, like all walks of life, is full of different, sometimes contrasting, personalities and philosophies, it's illuminating to see that certain consistencies keep reappearing.

There were, for instance, very few people I talked to who did not mention at least once how much they loved the sport. Figure skating has a certain, as sportswriter Cam Cole describes it, "brutality" to it that requires an equal degree of passion to overcome. When all else fails, skaters always try to rediscover their basic pleasure in the act of skating.

It's interesting to note that the Battle of the Brians is still with Brian Boitano and Brian Orser today. How could it not be? It was the best head-to-head duel of our time. More interesting is the sense of awe each man feels while watching the current crop of stars. Each wonders how he actually managed to get through something so pressure-packed as Calgary 1988.

Liz Manley and Barbara Ann Scott marvel at how an Olympic title can mean a lifetime of fame in two countries.

Janet Knight and Joanne Vincent, although they grew up 20 years, 3,000 miles (4 800 km) and two countries apart, felt similar ambivalences when they were touring with major ice shows: they were appalled by the weight-control problems and thrilled by the intensity of the overall experience.

Many skaters mentioned the "what-if?" concept. The great athletes have a sense of *carpe diem*—seize the day; they are terrified of being chained to the "what-if?" for the rest of their lives, although even with the great ones, circumstances can be out of their control. Injuries, illnesses, emotional downs, can all strike at precisely the wrong moment, and that is a recurring theme in every athlete's life.

Tara Lipinski and Audrey Thibault—14 and 10, respectively, when they spoke the words in this book—both insisted that they were not unlike other kids their age. "Just Tara, skater" is how Lipinski says she would describe herself. Debbi Wilkes, herself an international star at age 13, felt the same way back in the early 1960s: she thought it was normal to travel, compete and be well-known. It was only years later that she began to feel a little differently about her experiences.

It is that perspective of time that permits the older speakers to give eloquent voice to what it was that they went through. Even at 16, Michelle Kwan shows an understanding and maturity that would have been well out of her range the year before—the year she was World champion.

To anyone who knows these subjects, their tone and inflections should be instantly recognizable. You should be able to *hear* them. I can. Every one of them. From the lilting Julie Marcotte, to the matter-of-fact John Nicks. From the halting, tearful Marina Zoueva to the upbeat Kurt Browning. From the businesslike David Dore and Morry Stillwell to the grief-stricken Frank Carroll and Tracy Wilson.

And there *is* grief in this book. "Talking about it" is one of the accepted stages in coping with tragedy. After many rereadings, I can still barely get through the memories of Tracy Wilson and Marina Zoueva without crying. And isn't that what real communication is about? What voices are for? To make us feel what the other person feels, know what the other person knows?

All these interviews were recorded on tape, some by phone, most in person. In a few instances, but only a few, there was some substantial prodding via the question-and-answer format. Most often, speakers would begin slowly, warm to their subject and gallop away. Their thoughts and observations were transcribed into print, with little editing, except for space. You could argue that it is unfair to a Philippe Candeloro or a Marina Zoueva—both of whom, under less passionate circumstances, speak impeccable English—not to have rearranged their words into grammatically correct English. To have done so, however, would have lost the sense of "being there." It would have foolishly abandoned the presence of Voice.

Some speakers appear in this book more than once, and for that I make no apology. When you have access to observations on a variety of topics from a Toller Cranston, a Robin Cousins, a Michael Rosenberg or a Brian Orser, you do not stand on ceremony.

These are voices that are spoken from the routineness of skating's business offices and from the ruthless excitement of the arena, from the peaks of Mount Olympus and the valleys of hospital emergency rooms.

These are the Voices of the sport we love.

The Five
Rings of Fame

BRIAN BOITANO

The Battle of the Brians

There may have been better skates, or more great skates on a single evening, than on February 20, 1988, at the Calgary Saddledome, but history has never presented us with performances that lived up to—no, surpassed—the hype and hysteria of the Battle of the Brians.

Tonya Harding and Nancy Kerrigan had more hype leading up to the Lillehammer Games, but didn't come close to rising to the occasion on the ice. The skating may have been better at the 1996 World Championships, but it was not encumbered by remotely the same kind of expectations laid upon Brian Boitano and Brian Orser.

The evidence was all there to see. Under enormous pressure, Brian Boitano was brilliant that night, and he won a tenth-of-a-point decision over his Canadian rival.

With hard work and an unswerving belief in his coach, Linda Leaver, and his new choreographer, Sandra Bezic, Boitano had reworked himself as a skater for the 1988 Olympic season. He was more self-assured on the ice, and had made the leap from technician to performer. He no longer withdrew from the audience but reached out. And when he added a perfectly suited style to his consistently precise jumps, he became a formidable foe—and an Olympic champion.

After Calgary, Boitano established new standards for professional skating, routinely landing triple Axels and triple–triple combinations on tour. He was unbeatable in professional competitions for five years, and when the "Boitano Rule" was passed by the ISU, permitting pros to return to amateur ranks, he qualified for the 1994 Olympic Games at Lillehammer. He fell on a triple Axel in the short program and was not a factor in the competition.

Lillehammer was his third Olympics, but to most fans, there is only one that counts.

The Olympics are big. They're so big. The Battle of the Brians was really the hill, like the top of a bell curve, of my amateur skating. In 1984 I didn't really realize what it meant to be there. Sarajevo was, "Whoa, I'm at the Olympics. Whoa!" I wasn't skating my best, and I had a tough time. Brian Orser and I were doing triple Axels, but I just wasn't skating as well as I wanted to be. I ended up fifth, a placement that I'd dreamed about, but I still wasn't skating my very best. And I've wondered whether that took away from how I felt about the Olympics in Sarajevo. I was so worried about my skating that I couldn't enjoy the Olympic experience.

Then in 1988 I was skating exactly the way I wanted to. I felt great. I felt it was my Olympics. But with the Battle of the Brians, I felt I might have to put in four more years. I knew I had to be perfect to even come close to beating Brian Orser. I felt at my peak. I think the timing of my amateur career was really right. It's hard to sustain over two Olympics. I think it's really hard to skate at the top of your game for four years and then win the Olympics.

I have complete respect for Brian Orser for being second at two Olympics. I think Canadians were pretty hard on him . . . but he was great in the Olympics.

Nineteen eighty-eight changed my life. I came out of the Olympic Village and people knew who I was. So many people did not know me when I went into the Olympic Village. Peter Oppegard was my roommate in Calgary and he went back to the States right after I skated to do a TV show, and when he returned he said, "I think maybe you should prepare yourself for what's happening in America. Because everyone knows who you are."

When I got off the plane in San Francisco I was surrounded by FBI and police people. It was incredible—it was wild. It takes a long time to adjust to it. It's life changing.

It's not a gradual thing with skaters. In America, it's a thing where one day happens and you become well-known and you have to deal with. And it never dies down for athletes in America. Once you have it you have it for the rest of your life, and you either adjust to it or you freak out because of it.

I watch these guys skate today and I think, "It's incredible that I went out there and I did that." Watching Elvis skate his very best, I say, "That was me." I skated my very best and I did it when it was really important for me to do it.

Nobody knew who I was in March of 1987. Nobody. Even right before the Olympics, there was a lot of hype about the Battle of the Brians, but if you'd walked down the street and said Brian Boitano, maybe some people would have known, but not many.

It still affects me, and it frustrates me a lot of times. Athletes are different than a lot of other celebrities in America. For one thing, they know you as Brian Boitano, not as a character you portray. Actors are their characters. Singing stars are their songs. For another, athletes represent their country. People feel they have part of them, which is great. They feel they know them because of all the up-close-and-personals they've seen year-in and year-out. I think it's a real responsibility.

In 1994 when I decided to go back to the Olympics, I felt I'd done everything I could as a professional and needed a challenge. I just wish that my body had felt better and it had been more fair to me. I never let anyone know how badly injured my knee was.

I skated first in the short program. I opened with a triple Lutz and then I went into the triple Axel, and it was the weirdest thing. When I stepped forward on the left foot, I felt this hand pushing on my chest. It was almost spiritual. I felt this something holding me, and as I was coming down toward the landing I could hear myself say, "Arrrrgggh" because I was trying so hard to squeeze in to get the rotation, but I felt something dragging me. It was a spiritual experience.

I've made only two mistakes in my life in a short program, and that was one. I spent the whole rest of the program going, "There's a reason for this and I'm going to know someday." But I don't know yet. I think it was a way of keeping me from something I wasn't supposed to do.

I'm glad of the short-program mistake in this way only—my knee was so bad all year I could only practice two triple Lutzes a day and two flips a day. But the mistake was on the Axel, which the knee didn't bother me on. If it had been on the flip or something I would have said, "I shouldn't have come back." So it didn't make me feel stupid that I came back when my body hurt.

You know the kids' game where you take plastic and write on it, then lift the plastic and it's erased? I feel that 1994 was like that to the American public. They don't even remember that I was in the Lillehammer Games. The Tonya–Nancy thing was part of that—they were so focused on that.

I think the other thing was that Americans kind of held me up after 1988 in this place of esteem. But I think my interviews after I didn't skate well in 1994 were really what made them like me as a person. "Oh, he's handling it so well."

That's very important to the American public. Look what happened to Nancy Kerrigan. It's almost more important than the fact that you're successful.

BRIAN ORSER

Which Brian Are You?

No Canadian athlete has ever faced more pressure than Brian Orser did during the 1988 Calgary Olympics. He was the only legitimate gold medal hope his country had in the only Winter Games ever to be held in Canada. While hockey players may have faced enormous expectations in the Canada Cup and Stanley Cup, they at least had teammates to depend upon.

Orser was the reigning World champion, having beaten Brian Boitano in Cincinnati in 1987, after Boitano had won in Geneva the previous season when Orser fell attempting a combination that had never been accomplished—a triple Axel–triple toe loop—and his program unraveled.

Ironically, for the man whose name was synonymous with the triple Axel, it was a triple Axel not attempted that probably cost him the closest men's Olympic event in history. Orser was the first skater to land two triple Axels in the same program, but at Calgary he didn't attempt the second one, and in the interview that follows he explains why.

Since the celebrated Battle of the Brians, one of the few megahyped sporting events that actually lived up to its billing, Orser has had a successful professional career. He starred in both American and Canadian versions of Stars on Ice until 1997, when he took part in only the Canadian tour. He, Brian Boitano and Katarina Witt won Emmys for their work in Carmen on Ice. He has had several critically acclaimed television specials of his own, does a number of charity functions each year, is the only skater to be named an Officer of the Order of Canada and, as Toller Cranston says, "is one of the nicest people in skating—sometimes too nice for his own good."

But he is brutally honest in admitting that while the pain of losing the Battle of the Brians has receded, it never completely goes away.

Canadian skating is indebted to Brian Orser. He, Barbara Underhill, Paul Martini, Tracy Wilson and Rob McCall rescued the sport in Canada when it had become a competitive wasteland. And not enough of the current generation of skaters understand what they owe to Orser and Boitano for having the courage to stand and deliver that brilliant week in February.

It wasn't as though it was overwhelming, I knew it was going to be big. I was exactly where I wanted to be. I didn't want to go into the Olympics as anything other than World champion. And with that came everything else—all the media and all the expectations of being Canada's only World champion, in any sport, at Calgary. So you were not just king of the Canadian skating heap, but the whole Canadian sports heap. It was extra pressure, but that was fine.

Brian and I were always very friendly, from the time we went to Junior Worlds and onward. There was obviously a rivalry, but 1982, '83, '84, '85 I never considered him *the* rival because there were some people between us—Alexander Fadeev, Norbert Schramm, Josef Sabovcik. So I never considered him a head-to-head rival, although I considered him a very good skater. Then 1986 happened, although I still won the freestyle that year. And then he became a serious contender.

We always joked around that I was older than him. Even in Olympic year, he sent me a very funny birthday card about being old. And it was a joke. It wasn't a little dig or anything.

I think Brian is absolutely right. We are much better friends now than we were then. We were friendly—I never disliked him. But I always kept a close eye on him. In 1987 and 1988 I tried to focus in on what he was doing and to justify why I was better, justify why my program was better. And up until 1988 I always had better programs, until he moved over to Sandra [Bezic] and she developed the whole package. And that paid off for him in a huge way—not in just the better program, but in confidence and going out on the ice like a World champion.

In the free skate, I think Brian skated first in the final group and I skated third or fourth. I knew he skated well, and I had learned from other years to not ignore it.

I remember sitting up in the stands during practice with Barbie Underhill after the short program and I saw on her lap a sheet with the order of elements, and she had Brian's page flipped open. As I was talking to her I looked down, and she didn't have the second triple Axel listed. That's one of the reasons I didn't think he was going to do a second triple Axel, and when I went out there I didn't know he'd done it. I think this is the first time I've told anybody, but that was one of the reasons I didn't put it in. I remember thinking, "Just be safe." I'd had that one little mess-up with the flip, so [I told myself] "Do as clean a program as you possibly can." I thought with each of us doing one Axel, I would probably have enough to win. It would have been a tossup, but I was World champion and we were in Canada, and that was going to weigh the scale my way. If I hadn't looked at the list, I would have gone for it.

At first, I said it was fine that I didn't win, that life would go on, blah, blah, blah. And life did go on. The first couple of years as a pro, people would come up and say, "Which Brian are you?" And that was great.

But then as time goes on, you're still living with the fact that you came second twice at the Olympics. So close each time. And it's something that haunts you every day—"What if I'd won? How would my life be different?"

That was the time, but it didn't happen. And it's taken me a long while to get over it. Living through Rob's [McCall] sickness and his death, and with my mom dying, that kind of stuff sometimes helps. To see that [losing is] not everything. I've got my health. I still get to do a sport I love. So I'm not closing the show every time. Oh, well.

But it took me a long time. And still it's hard, still I catch myself going, "What if?" I still try to justify to myself that I've got two Olympic silver medals and a World Championship, to justify the eight Canadian titles.

I used to think, "World title, Olympic title, kinda the same." But it's not. The Olympic title is it.

It. It. It.

The Battle of the Brians saved my butt, professionally. Everyone remembers it, and that helped me a lot.

We pushed each other to go out and do it, to produce that night of skating. When it comes down to it, we did exactly everything that was expected. It would have been a drag if one of us had missed something in the short program. All the wind would have been out of the sails and it would have been just another event. But this one was back and forth. He was second, I was third, in figures. I was first, he was second, in the short.

I think to the general public [the closeness] gave skating more credibility. It wasn't as if someone was just going to come in and twirl his way to the top. There was a fierce battle going on. Every step of the way was important that year—what you said, what you did, how many hours you trained, what type of program, type of costume. It did lift [skating] to another level, because that was when "the package" became important. You had to do everything. That was the start of the boom.

I realize now what we went through. I'll see a skater out there at Olympics or World Championships in the warm-up and I'll wonder, "How are these guys out there? How do they do it?" Not because they're so good, but because there's all that pressure and they still have to go out and do it.

And I realize that only 10 years ago I was doing it, being the guy everyone in the warm-up was watching. Every second of that warm-up in 1988, people were either looking at Brian or looking at me.

BARBARA ANN SCOTT-KING

The Golden Age of Skating

The Golden Age of North American figure skating—which is still with us—officially began in St. Moritz, Switzerland, in 1948. Skating, like most facets of cultural life, had been interrupted by World War II, and there had not been a Winter Olympics since the Garmisch Games of 1936.

Prior to the war, Europeans had dominated the international competitions; no North American had ever won a World Championship or Olympic gold medal. But with Americans still being able to train—although on a limited basis—during the war, while many European rinks were destroyed or taken over for other purposes, the balance of power was bound to shift.

And shift it did. The two singles events at St. Moritz were won by North Americans. Barbara Ann Scott, the Canadian flag bearer in the opening ceremonies, was the women's champion and American Dick Button began his legendary reign in the men's event. When the World Championships had resumed in Stockholm the year before, the two North American youngsters had served notice that they would be among the favorites for the St. Moritz Olympics. Button was silver medalist behind Hans Gerschwiler and Scott became the first non-European to win a World title in any discipline, triggering a skating boom in North America and a nation's love affair with her that has not abated.

A half century after she conquered the hearts of two continents, Barbara Ann Scott is still the queen of Canadian skating. And that's despite living in Chicago for more than four decades with her husband, Tom King. She has never lost touch with the Canadian skating fraternity, and is a frequent visitor to major competitions in her native country. And she has never stopped being Barbara Ann Scott: bubbly, witty, accessible, kind and elegant.

She was elected to the World Figure Skating Hall of Fame in 1979, three years after Button.

I can't believe that people still care so much about the Olympic victory, and I'm very humbled by that.In those days, St. Moritz was where all the royalty went for vacation. It still had that wonderful old-Swiss-village feel to it. The school figures were done on the ice rink at the old Palace Hotel. The free skating was down the hill, on a big, outdoor, hockey-sized rink. When you looked up into the village there was a little church just above the main street, and that will always be special to me, because just before the Olympics, one of our Canadian hockey players married a Danish girl and they didn't have any close friends, so I was her maid of honor in that little church. [In fact,] there's a poster of me being judged doing school figures and in the background you can see that little church.

When Sheldon Galbraith came to coach me, he did my program with different cuts of music, and this was a big innovation. We were the first people to bring cuts of music over to Europe. In the old-fashioned way, you just put a record on, and if you finished skating before the record ended, they just took it off. Or if the record finished before you did, they put it back on.

When the record was being played, your trainer was right there to make sure that it was all right. I started my program from a standstill, with three Axels into a back sit spin. The sound of the music went jump–jump–jump–spin. Well, in Prague [at the 1948 European Championships, for which North Americans were then eligible] when I got into the back sit spin, the music went *w-h-h-h-r-r-r-u-u-p-p-p*. The needle had flown off. I had to think pretty fast. Do I keep going? Do I stop? And what will the judges think? So I stopped, and they started the record again.

The year before St. Moritz was the first Europeans and Worlds since the war. The rude awakening came when we first went down to practice and the wind was blowing as we tried to do school figures. I'd always been, as Otto Gold called it, a "hothouse skater," so it was a very strange feeling to adapt to the outdoors. You planned your school figures so that if there was a wind, hopefully it would blow you back to center. At those first Worlds in 1947, we did six figures, on both feet. There were 20-some girls, so the figures took two days! The next year they changed it, so for the Olympics you did the six figures on alternate feet, and it took only one day.

When we went to do our school figures there had been a thaw, and they said,

"You can't do them today because the ice is too soft." You're all keyed up and ready to go, so that was a letdown. We had to go back the next day.

The following day was the free skating. They had played two championship hockey games on the ice in the morning and they couldn't flood or do anything to the ice because the weather was too mild. So Sheldon and I skated the whole surface, looking for the worst ruts and holes so I wouldn't do the jumps and spins there.

After the marks came out and I had won, it was almost a letdown after all the hard work. All of a sudden it was over. The Canadian hockey team, who had also won the Olympic gold, scooped me up, carried me around on their shoulders and gave me a chocolate bar. To this day, I live on chocolate.

When I got back to Canada, the welcome was wonderful. We stopped in several cities because they were planning receptions. In Halifax it was two in the morning or something, but there were a whole lot of people waiting and cheering. Toronto had a reception outside city hall, and [it was reported that] there were 60,000 people there.

People seemed to be very excited about the Olympics. In Canada, it was very special because I was the first one to bring back a gold. We're a smaller country than the United States and I think the country was just happy that a Canadian had done something. And I was young, so that added something, too. In Europe, [the Games were] something cheerful after the war, and people were looking for something to be happy about.

I had so many good-luck wishes before and after the championship. That's why, when I'm in a Canadian city, I like to go into retirement homes or veterans homes and see these people who were so good to me. They may be old and forgotten, but to me they're very important.

The most important thing about skating is that it teaches you to do the things you *should* do before you do the things you *want* to do. And I think perhaps [that self-discipline is] a little lacking nowadays.

I hope athletes today recognize what a privilege it is to represent their country. God gave them the talent to use, and they're obligated to develop it. Someone else wasn't given this talent.

To carry your country's flag, especially in the Olympics, is the greatest honor and privilege an athlete can have.

TODD ELDREDGE

Okay, This Is the Big One

The Winter Games are the great carrot on the end of figure skating's stick. Despite the increased financial value of fall internationals and the World Championships—and despite the fact that the Olympics don't offer formal prize money—most career decisions are still based on the four-year cycle that rules the sport far more than any skating official would care to admit.

Todd Eldredge's return to prominence has been one of the most gratifying comeback stories in this decade. He had won two U.S. titles and a World bronze medal by the time he was 20. But in the 1991–92 season, years of jarring jumps finally caught up to him, and a misaligned spinal joint ruined his training for the Albertville Games. Because of his world standing he was given a berth on the U.S. team despite missing nationals due to the injury, but he didn't make his double Axel in the short program and finished 10th overall.

After that, he sensed that two other skaters—Scott Davis and Mark Mitchell—had captured the favor of the American skating fraternity, and it affected his competitive psyche. He finished a terrible sixth at the U.S. nationals. The following season, the Lillehammer Olympic year, he was skating well, but developed a fever during nationals and finished fourth. Davis and Brian Boitano were the Olympic representatives, and Davis and Aren Nielsen made up the World team.

But since then it has been blue skies for this soft-spoken son of a fisherman. He won three fall internationals to open the 1994–95 season, and recaptured his national crown, the first time an American had regained a title after three years off the podium. He followed up with a solid silver at Worlds, then won that title the next year. The year after that, he took silver again, despite an ankle injury a few weeks before the event.

Todd Eldredge had clearly fought his way back, and a large part of his motivation came from his Olympic disappointments.

At the Worlds, everyone's intensity goes up maybe 10 percent. Olympics is very similar that way. But it comes around every four years, so that makes it much more important, much more interesting, as far as the skaters are concerned. When it does come around again, you feel, "Okay, this is the Big One."

In 1992 I had the back injury. Coming off a bronze medal in the Worlds, you're considered, supposedly, a contender for a medal in the Olympics. But the injury was there, so the medal picture was gone. The back was so bad I didn't skate at U.S. nationals. Between nationals and Olympics I was staying in Worcester, Mass., visiting my doctor there and feeling pretty good. But the trip to Albertville was a nightmare. It took us at least 13 hours, once we landed, to get into the Village because of all the accreditation and the different things we had to do. During the flight over, my back started acting up a bit, so that wasn't too exciting, to say the least.

I took it a little easy when I first got there. Kind of, "Okay, it will go away. It will go away. It's getting better." I had to take a lot of therapy. It did still hurt when I skated, but it wasn't real bad. I think it was more asking "Is it going to hurt when I do something?" that kind of throws off your timing on different elements. I think that was a lot of it. And I ended up 10th.

I didn't feel a lot of pressure because I decided to go and Mark Mitchell then couldn't. I knew that when I left, my back was feeling pretty good, so I knew I'd made the right decision. Other people maybe didn't think so—you know, "If you're not 100 percent, then you shouldn't be here." I felt that I'd earned it with some of the things that I'd done previously. Obviously, everybody wants to go to the Olympics. That was my first opportunity to do something like that, so I said, "My back's feeling good. Let's go for it."

In 1993, things were going so poorly that I almost quit. But another Olympics was only a year away, so I said, "Well, let's give it another shot." It comes down to nationals—that famous week [Harding–Kerrigan] in Detroit—and I come down with the flu, a 104 temperature, and that didn't make things too exciting for me. I skated, but didn't skate that well because I couldn't breathe. And I didn't make the Olympic team.

It was very disappointing. But I knew that if I hadn't been sick I would have been there because of the way that I'd skated previous to the nationals.

I think that, and another Olympics, kind of kept me going from '94 to now.

CAROL HEISS-JENKINS

A Rare Case of Not Touring

Later generations will recognize her as the coach of Tonia Kwiatkowski, Timothy Goebel and a host of other high-profile skaters, or as a spokesperson for various commercial products.

But Carol Heiss was the first American woman to win an Olympic skating championship in her home country when she took gold at Squaw Valley in 1960. That capped an incredible career that included five World titles—a total surpassed only by the great Sonja Henie—four American crowns and a silver medal at the 1956 Cortina Olympics when she was just 16. Three months after the Squaw Valley Games, she married Hayes Alan Jenkins, who also knew a thing or two about the podium: he won four World titles and was 1956 Olympic champion.

Heiss may be the only Olympic champion who never toured after her victory. "I just couldn't see doing that," she said. She opted, instead, to star in the movie Snow White and the Three Stooges. *She had a seven-year contract to do more movies, but she and Jenkins started a family. She became heavily involved in raising their three children and volunteering in hospitals and for women's organizations—"All the things I never had a chance to do when I was skating."*

She didn't go into coaching until 18 years after her Olympic victory, and works out of the Winterhurst Figure Skating Club in Lakewood, Ohio.

Where, it seems, not everyone knows of her golden past.

The funniest thing is the woman who came into Winterhurst and didn't know who I was. Somebody happened to say I was in the Olympics, so she introduced herself and said, "How did you do?" I said, "Well, I got the silver medal." And she said, "Oh, that's too bad…what did you go on to do after that?" I said, "Oh, I stayed in." And she said, "Well, did you make the Olympics again?" And I said, "Yes, and I won the gold."

And immediately, the whole tone changed. She wanted my autograph. She said, "What's your name again?" It made all the difference in the world. Gold. Five World titles and a silver didn't mean a thing. I said to her after, "I'm very proud of my silver medal in 1956. First time I made the Olympic team and I'm on the podium."

I think it's more like that in the United States, but it's worldwide, too. They never say, "Olympic champion," which is interesting. Most of the time it's, "I got the gold." I don't know why that is. For years I just said, "Olympic champion." I think that TV has done a lot in that area, sort of the slogan "Go for the gold," and I think the general public is geared to that more now.

In Cortina in 1956, I had my 16th birthday and the U.S. team gave me a party one evening in the hotel, which was really exciting.

The difference physically between the two Olympics was that in Cortina we didn't really have an Olympic village. That was still the era when the teams had their own hotels. I remember the American team having a small hotel on the corner of one of the main streets leading up to the stadium. The whole team—the skiers, the speed skaters, the figure skaters, the ski jumpers, the hockey team—stayed together in the same hotel.

In Squaw Valley we had an Olympic village. It gave it a different feel. You were still with athletes and a team, but I just thought it was a lot of fun being around a lot of other countries. Pretty soon, I was listening to stories from hockey players from Germany or Norwegian ski jumpers. Most of the Europeans could speak English.

And the Russians were new at that point. I don't think there were any Russian skaters in 1956, but in Squaw Valley there were the Zhuks, and it was kind of fun to talk to them. It was height of the Cold War, and it was my first real exposure to Russians. The Worlds aren't the same as Olympics that way. At Worlds you go in and it's much more "the American team," "the Canadian team." Whereas in the Olympics you have much more of a concept that you're doing this for your country and that all the countries are involved. You're sharing things, and it's very special. It was more fun in Squaw Valley in that sense.

Personally, I enjoyed 1956 more…until Squaw Valley was over, of course, and I'd won it. But not knowing what an Olympic Games was like, marching in for the first time in the parade, was, as the kids say now, "Awesome." Making the team for the first time, getting the silver medal—it was all very exciting. I had no real expectations of myself.

In 1960, it was much more nerve-racking for me, much more of a business kind of competition. It was a business venture. I'd already been four-time World champion, three-time national champion. And having just won my national title a month before Squaw Valley, at that point my expectations were very high.

It wasn't at all the way it is today, with so much resting on [winning]. Yes, you could be the star of an ice show—if I'd done it, it would have been the

Carol Heiss Ice Revue, just as it was the Barbara Ann Scott Ice Revue—but I decided to do the movie, instead.

I did get some commercials, I did do some endorsing of products for about five years, and then I was a spokeswoman for several companies and did that for nearly 20 years. And I don't think that would have come along if I hadn't been Olympic champion. And remember, this was an American winning in the United States, and that made a big difference. I think if it had been Europe or the Orient, [the win] wouldn't have had the same impact. It was the first Olympics in America since Lake Placid [1932] and also the first on live television.

I decided to do the movie because you could make more money in a shorter time, but I wasn't committed to being an actress. I wanted to live in Akron—Hayes was a lawyer there—and I needed time to be a somewhat normal person. I was ready for that.

TOLLER CRANSTON

We Are All Humans Here

To say that Toller Cranston has marched to the beat of his own drummer does not begin to do justice to percussion or to the man himself. Although he never won a World title—in fact, has won only a solitary World medal, the bronze in 1974—no one of his era, and very few of any era, has influenced skating as much as Cranston has. Athletes who were not even born when he was engaged in his furious battles against the constraints and prejudices of amateur skating say that he's their favorite skater of all time. The unique interpretation of music, the distortions of line, the counterattack on the way things had always been done—these are all Cranston legacies.

The International Skating Union, and sometimes his own association in Canada, never knew quite what to make of Cranston. It's to the ISU's great shame that it never found a way to make him a champion, because—on the ice, at least—he represented what skating could have been 20 years earlier had it cast off the anchor of its archaic past. Sometimes, when it seemed that the climate was right for him to win, he would make technical mistakes; sometimes, when he was absolutely on top of his game, the political winds blew stiffly against him.

Depending upon whom you talk to, he was robbed by the judges—who often hid behind the evil cloak of figures—many times, but Cranston feels that only in his last amateur competition, the 1976 Worlds, was it blatant larceny. He had won the bronze medal at the Olympics, but was kept off the podium at Worlds.

He left amateur skating bitter at the politics and the lack of vision, and did not hesitate to vent that bitterness while pursuing a fabulous pro career that is still ongoing. But at the 1997 Worlds in Lausanne, he was the ISU's honored guest. His paintings, huge canvases of exploding color, adorned the International Olympic Museum during the Worlds.

You could write a book about Cranston—in fact, he's just written one about himself: Zero Tollerance—*and not cover everything. He inspires and irritates; he attracts and threatens; he challenges every assumption you've ever held about the sport, about art, about living.*

One memorable late afternoon, he sat against the garden window of the lobby bar of the Royal Savoy Hotel in Lausanne and read to us from his memoirs, pausing for effect... and to make sure we were paying absolute attention. And he touched only upon funny bits, because it was a day of warmth and friendship. The book is also full of the deep, dark valleys of a self-absorbed artist. An editor had suggested he subtitle the book Chronicles of a Misspent Life, *to which he replied, "How dare you? My life has not been misspent. My life has been textured."*

He told me that that insult jolted him into a clarity about himself. "So now, rather than 'Poor little me, isn't it too bad that this didn't happen and that didn't happen,' I'm thinking for the first time, 'Lucky me.'"

Lucky us. I asked him to speak about his Olympic experience, and he did. Sort of. What follows is allegedly Cranston on the Olympics. But it's really Cranston on the human journey.

Irony of ironies, I am the paid guest of the ISU. I can go into the lounge and eat their hors d'oeuvres and drink their wine and sit down with them and they have to talk to me... I have access to the inner sanctuary.

And I don't know if this is because I've sort of grown up, but if I was their enemy and they were my enemy, what you do find out at the end of the day is that everyone's just a human being. That awful, horrible Dr. Didec, who gave me a 5.2 in the Olympics and cost me ninth place? You can sit down and he can shed tears over his brother-in-law who just died. In other words, the element of being a human is the glue that binds us all. Even with Carlo Fassi, who was always teaching my enemies, my competition. The day before he died we had a very intense, pleasant, man-to-man talk about everything as two humans, and not as coach and competitor. Sitting next to Cinquanta at the dinner, having chats with Samaranch—it was all so strange to me. Actually rather funny.

The chessboard can be wiped clean—different power structures, a change of the guard. If certain other people were still in charge of the ISU—Sonia Bianchetti being one—I wouldn't have that [outlook]. But things change.

God did not want me to win the Olympics. I'm convinced of that. I also know that you cannot make a cheap deal with God. He's not into it. And you can't choose the color of your medal.

And He really helped me by not winning, because if I'd won, I'd be even more unbearable than I am now. I had to learn that humility. I had to eat humble pie and I had to spend 20 or 25 years proving that I was really a good skater.

And then you meet, over all those years, people who put you in that position, who cost you that title. But I must say for the record that John Curry's win [1976 Olympics] was absolutely uncontested. It was a great win.

There's a hang-up—that mushroom cloud that hangs over your life, where you can't undo the past and you can't reskate that performance and you can't change things. You have to live with it. It's a festering albatross around your neck that starts to smell even more the longer you have it. Rather than evaporating and not smelling, it becomes worse.

Insecurity, a sense of one's personal failure, is all part of the trappings of your professional life and image. Which, I suspect, with my flamboyant, over-the-top, fur-coats-dragging-on-the-ground image was all really just an excuse to say, "You know, guys, I really am good. Look at me." I suspect that.

But the bitterness, truly the last drop of it, has finally evaporated, and it really happened in Lausanne. When you see people who have done things to you over the past sitting down at the next table, it can have a boost of adrenaline, or emotion or energy or passion, that kind of comes right up in your throat. Then you're not over it. But if you can see those players and feel nothing, you're over it. It's the first time that's happened. I'm not happy about it. I'm just acknowledging it. And it's probably good.

I've kind of come into the inner sanctuary with a different color of credential, which is "professional spectator and artist." I watch skating and yet I feel estranged from it. I asked Krisztina Regoeczy, who was the World champion [ice dancing] in 1980, "When you're watching skaters, do you feel you want to jump out on the ice and say, 'People, look at me'?" And she said, "No, I don't."

And I said, "I used to, and this is the first time I haven't," so I think that's out of me, too.

I think one of the secrets of life and growing up, something [that gives] people a huge advantage if they're able to do it, is to see things as they really are when they're happening. For example, the Duchesnays. For all the success they had, skating gave them no pleasure. Skating was torture for them. If you can enjoy whatever it is for the moment, when it's happening, that's really one of the secrets.

To say that I enjoyed my life, enjoyed my skating career? I have ambivalent feelings about that. I don't know whether I did. I always thought I didn't. I've had highs and lows, and horizontal extremes and everything else. I've done and seen it all. Actually, now I think I've lived a very privileged life. I think I've been lucky. You have a bus driver, say, who might think your career is far superior to his own, in a way. But [you don't] think that way. That's often the case with people who have achieved great renown. We want the pat on the head. People might think, "Well, you're this and you're that and you've done this and you've done that, like wow." But it's the human part of you that is really somewhat enduring. Let's say I'm talking to Christopher Dean. "Excuse me, but I just want you to know that you're my favorite skater and you're just wonderful. I hope it doesn't bother you." If Christopher said, "Yes, it does bother me," he'd be lying. Because all those people who have achieved things really want to be appreciated.

I don't lust after mass love, but I would really like the ISU—this is how sick it is. I mean, I should be so above it—to say, "You know, we didn't really understand you when we were judging you, and you really were a great skater and we just wanted you to know that." It would be like snipping the cord of the albatross around my neck and I would be free of that burden forever.

Because the human side of you always thinks that [people] don't think you're any good, or you didn't do anything, or you're a failure.

It's because we're human beings.

ROBIN COUSINS

A Dissenting Opinion

To the casual fan, Robin Cousins is best known as the 1980 Olympic champion. But it is quite obvious that's not how he wishes to be solely, or even primarily, remembered.

He's far more passionate about discussing his wide variety of professional skating endeavors—including the elaborate rebirth of the old theater-on-ice concept through adaptations of modern musicals such as Starlight Express*—or his pursuit of the flawless program than he is about the gold medal he won at Lake Placid in 1980. The defining moment of his amateur career may have come not on the Olympic podium but at the World Championships three weeks later, with the perfect symbiosis between audience and performer. Lake Placid, where he won, served a practical function. Dortmund, where he did not, served a metaphysical one.*

Still, as one of only three men who have won an Olympics but not a Worlds, Cousins is a metaphor for the fact that the Winter Games are an altogether different fortnight.

I suppose. Everybody considers the Olympics *the* event. I still bitterly regret not having a World Championship title. Not for want of trying, I hasten to add. Maybe the one I was supposed to have wasn't the one in 1980 but another, which I've often been told.

That one was in Ottawa in 1978, where we went to fourth places to determine the winner—who was Charlie Tickner, not to begrudge him a World title. I ended up losing a title by not having a majority of firsts and seconds but by having both, and having an eighth and a ninth from an East German and a Russian. It's just one of those uncanny results that make you go, "Whoa." And it was one of the best skates of my life.

At that time they were still giving out a gold medal for figures and a gold medal for free skate, and I have a World title for free skate—in fact, I have three. And they are as important to me as the Olympic gold, in my heart.

From a personal point of view, I know I would be talking here—having done some of the things that I've done in my career—whether I'd won that Olympic gold medal or not.

I've always said that the Olympic gold medal might have opened those doors, but it doesn't mean to say that I wouldn't have found the keys of my own volition had I not won. There are those people who live their lives with the be-all and end-all as the result of an event. I've never thought that way.

There have been lots of Olympic and World champions since me, but if I still want people to knock on my door or phone me up and say, "We want you to skate," I have to give them a reason other than the fact that I have an Olympic title. Why would they phone me, when they can phone Scott, Brian, Victor or Alexei? Just saying you are Olympic champion is not good enough.

I came off the ice at Lake Placid and said that my regret as Olympic champion was that I had not done it with a clean performance. I made a mistake near the beginning of the program—the triple loop was not clean. But then I put that out of my mind and, as Carlo Fassi said, I "sailed through the rest."

Fine, but it wasn't clean. And I went to Dortmund [the World Championship] saying I would skate clean and I did. I didn't win, but I was rewarded for that with all those 6.0s and an audience I will never forget. One of the German newspapers said there wasn't a florist in Germany that had flowers left by five o'clock that afternoon. I had buckets—five four-foot rubber trash cans full—of flowers.

My grandfather had died the year before and my grandmother came to the championships for the first time. Her first international event was my last. People would come up and ask me for my autograph and my grandmother's would already be there—"Granny Cousins." They were treating her with the same sort of reverence that people save for the Queen Mother. I have to say she reveled in it. It was wonderful that she would have the chance to experience that once.

I don't have a passion for the Olympics as an adventure, but I have a passion for ice skating. I didn't get into skating because of competition. I got into skating because I could play at being Gene Kelly. I wanted to *be* Gene Kelly when I was a kid.

For me now, to do some theater and be a good song-and-dance man is my dream come true. Winning the Olympics was not my dream come true.

It's like John Curry. The Olympics was his way of being able to do his art form in a way that he could get it seen. If there had been an alternative, I know he would have taken it.

And I might well have followed suit.

KURT BROWNING

The One That Got Away

Kurt Browning personifies all the unpredictability that makes the Olympics a different animal from the World Championships. Browning was clearly the skater of his time, the post–Calgary Games era. A month after the 1988 Olympics, he became the first skater to land a quadruple jump. A year after that, he won his first of four World Championships. A couple of years after that, he was being hailed as the most entertaining skater in the amateur world.

He is the only Canadian to win four World titles, the only skater ever to win a World title with and without compulsory figures. And he did each twice. He has dominated a season of professional competitions and is one of the preeminent skating showmen on the planet.

And yet in three Olympics, he never set foot on the podium. In the Calgary Games, he finished an encouraging eighth, a gateway to his World title the next season. But after winning three consecutive Worlds, he was stricken with a serious back injury for the 1991–92 season—an Olympic year. He missed the nationals and probably shouldn't have competed at Albertville, where he finished sixth.

And a disastrous short program took him out of the medal running—as it did fellow favorites Brian Boitano and Victor Petrenko—in Lillehammer two years later. That he could rally for a brilliant interpretation of his signature Casablanca free-skate program was a tribute to his pride and determination... and to the magnitude of the Olympic stage.

L ike Scott Hamilton says, the Olympics are just a whacky competition. I think it was different for me than it was for the typical "pin up pictures of figure skaters since you were five" kind of kid. I never did that. I never dreamed of the Olympics when I was eight. I started dreaming of the Olympics when someone told me, "Hey, when you turn senior and if you get top three you can go." Sounded good. I really just enjoyed, enjoyed, enjoyed. Because I didn't have any preconceived ideas of what the Olympics were supposed to be.

Calgary was the best. It was in my hometown and I had a couple of great skates. Everything was new...and great. But there was incredible pressure. The day of the short program, I was bawling at my practice. I could barely breathe.

I just wanted my coach to understand how scared I was and he kept denying it. "You're okay," [he'd say.] And I kept going, "No, I'm not okay. I'm scared like you wouldn't believe and I want you to acknowledge my fear." And once he sort of agreed with me that I was afraid and that I would be okay, then I started to *be* okay.

I was eighth and was incredibly happy with that. We thought it would be kind of neat to be in the top 10, but didn't think we would be. It set me off the next four years, and actually, it really set me off for the next month. I tried the quad in Calgary and had it for a second, but it slipped away and I fell. So we moved it to the first jump of the program at the World Championships at Budapest, and that was my only goal—to make that jump. And that's the one they counted as the first quad.

In 1992, I was injured. I was so "not-myself." I didn't want to carry the flag. I was sort of denying the importance of the event. I was frustrated at every practice. The ice was crap and terribly dangerous. I just remember never being able to get in a vibe. Basically, I guess, I should not have been there.

Yet I stepped on the ice and landed three triple Lutzes, and nothing else. It was Bizarro World. Everything was opposite. Here I am landing triple Lutz—I had trouble with that jump and I don't even do it any more—but not triple Axel. So Albertville was just goofy. It was a doomed year.

I apologized on the TV cameras afterward. I was just so sorry that that moment had come and gone and I hadn't dealt with it better on the ice. I was sorry that it hadn't been a better day. I was sorry that I let down a whole country—it was such a great opportunity to celebrate. When Ben Johnson won, I felt so Canadian . . . and then to have [my own] moment slip through my fingers . . . I was sorry. Everyone was saying I shouldn't have apologized, but if I wanted to apologize I should have been allowed to do that. I didn't go on and on about it.

I hadn't really lost before that—everything I had touched turned to gold. And then to go into Albertville . . . I just was lucky that I came across afterward.

Every ounce of my body wanted to turn pro. But then you go back to the rink and you think, "Hello! It's only two years until another Olympics. And I'm better than [I showed]." I knew it was my back that had kept me from skating well. Slipped disk. No training. A million excuses. I knew it wasn't me.

So I was looking forward to being me again, and that happened at the World Championships the next year in Prague. What a lot of people don't know is that I actually retired after Prague. I quit. I told the CFSA [Canadian Figure Skating

Association], told my parents, told my agent, told everyone. But I kind of got persuaded to come back.

Unfortunately for me, I think that I never truly came back. When I said I quit, I think that I actually did. So when I went to Lillehammer, I'm not sure that I had that fire, that focus, that killer thing.

I fell on a triple flip in the short. I made a mistake and I lost my edge and I fell. That's skating. But why did I single that double Axel at the end? Because I wasn't concentrating. I was feeling sorry for myself. I was thinking about Albertville, for God's sake. And then I did a single. I went, "Omigawd, I think that was a single. It *was* a single." I wasn't there. I was floating and I got what I deserved. I didn't even know until the next day that I was 12th.

I had a great long. I absolutely had to. I knew it was going to be my last amateur skate. I was okay with it because of something Brian Orser said once. He knew that Budapest [Worlds 1988] was going to be his last amateur skate and he was excited by the potential of going out great. And he had the skate of his life. I remember thinking at the time that someday I would have my last amateur skate, and I wanted to be like Brian. I wanted to go out confident.

And in this particular situation I really had no choice but to skate well. Because just the way people are going to look at me would be changed forever, and all that hard work I went through to win four World titles would be sort of, you know... tainted if I didn't pull off a great long program.

It was pretty damn inspired.

ELIZABETH MANLEY

The Night to Remember

Can you make a career in a single night? Elizabeth Manley did.

While everyone remembers the Battle of the Brians from the 1988 Olympics, everyone forgets that the Battle of the Carmens was supposed to be just as dramatic. Debi Thomas of the United States had won the World title in Europe in 1986; Katarina Witt of East Germany had won the World title in America in 1987. And they were both performing to Carmen *in the free skate. However, Thomas had a bad week. Witt was good enough, but not as good as she had been the year before, and the confrontation fizzled.*

But Manley, and to a lesser extent Midori Ito, rescued the women's event. Although she was a three-time national champion, she had never won a World medal. Burdened by serious bronchitis, a history of wearing her emotions on her sleeve and a habit of delivering either a good short program or a good long, but not both, Manley was given little consideration, probably justifiably, as an Olympic podium contender.

So her free-skate victory, which moved her up to the silver medal and nearly got her the gold, was the most unexpectedly spectacular performance in recent Olympic memory. From the moment she landed an early triple Lutz, the partisan audience at the Saddledome knew this was something special. Long before her music ended and she excitedly donned the white Stetson that had been flung onto the ice, 20,000 people were on their feet screaming.

And that white Stetson has become a symbol of what can be achieved on one special night.

To be pretty honest with you, the main objective with Calgary was to just get through it. About two and a half weeks before Calgary, we thought I was on the verge of pneumonia. The drug testing in skating is so severe that there was nothing that I was able to take to speed up the process of getting healthy. I remember Peter Dunfield [her coach] taking me to what I still to this day call a witch doctor. She was boiling red radish by my head because the aroma was to clear out my sinuses.

I had gone out to Calgary for the opening ceremonies and then come back home to Ottawa to train, and I was getting worse. I had about eight or nine days before I returned to Calgary, and I could not physically get through my programs. I was literally bedridden. There was nothing they could do.

The only way they could get me back to Calgary, because all the flights were booked solid, was by flying, I think it went, Ottawa to Toronto, Toronto to Thunder Bay, Thunder Bay to Regina, Regina into Calgary.

And nobody was talking about Elizabeth Manley.

The day before the figures, Katarina had a press conference in the morning and she had over a thousand people in there. A couple of hours later, Debi had hers and it was the same. Mine was after practice later in the afternoon and there were, like, nine reporters. All Canadians. I remember my heart sank I was so disappointed. I felt, nobody believes in me, right? Peter could see in my face how disappointed I was and he said, "Do you want this room filled like them? Then skate the way you can skate."

I was lucky, because once I started to get into the whole atmosphere of the Olympics and onto the ice, things started to improve. But my eardrums were still reversed and my balance was off, which was a real concern. Where it affected me most was in the figures. I had a real awkward time with them.

I remember crying after figures because I thought I hadn't done as well as I could have. Then, when they came into the dressing room for drug testing, they said, "You're sixth." I said, "What?"

It was the best I'd ever finished in figures, so I was already on a high. And then skating so well in the short program, actually getting the marks for it to finish third and feeling healthier every day—that was very good for me mentally.

I'd had problems before—in Cincinnati just the year before—in handling the pressure. I almost think that getting sick was a godsend for me because my body fighting [the illness] calmed me down. You know how hyper I get.

The night of the long program, I came in at the last minute. People were panicking at the building because I was so late, but I didn't want to be around the atmosphere long and get myself hyper and uptight. I really wasn't as nervous as I should have been or had been in the past—because the objective was just to get through the number.

It's really weird, but I don't remember anything about the program. I don't remember actually doing anything. I watch the tapes today...and it was a great number. The fast part was "The Night They Invented Champagne." How appropriate, eh? I didn't even bow at the end. I was just in shock.

The first thing I wanted to do was get to Peter and Sonya [Dunfield] and then find my mom. I didn't know how to handle how well I skated and the reaction. The crowd never sat down. They were going crazy. I just remember shaking and being in total disbelief that after the hell we went through for three weeks that I could have done the best ever.

At that point, people were thinking I had actually won the Olympics because I had won the free skate. I said, "This isn't happening." Peggy Fleming was interviewing me and people were grabbing me. "You gotta go here. You gotta go there." Even Katarina tells me to this day that when she was in the dressing room, she thought I had won. She came running out to find out what was going on. She had gone in to change and to watch Debi. I don't think she even watched me—that's how much people didn't expect me to be there.

Of course the press room after the long program was just jammed, standing room only. And no one, except the Canadians, had a story on me. All of a sudden you're looking at 800 press people in a panic. That was one of the greatest moments of the Olympics for me.

I think the Olympics made Liz Manley as a skater. I had a good record with internationals and nationals, but everybody always says an Olympic medal will give you a career, and it definitely has.

I think back on it all the time. Even on the days when I'm complaining about the schedule, I thank my lucky stars. My mom and I are in our house, and it's our first single home since the 1970s.

And it's all because of that night. And I'm so thankful.

Life ... and Death

TRACY WILSON

Facing the Truth

Skating has been affected more than any other sport by the AIDS epidemic. It has lost some of its brightest lights to the disease.

One of those was Rob McCall, who died in the fall of 1991. Creative, exuberant, extraordinarily witty, McCall was a true gem, and his death left a gaping hole in the lives of scores of people. Not the least of them was his partner of 10 years, Tracy Wilson.

The couple revitalized ice dancing in Canada, winning a bronze at the 1988 Calgary Olympics—Canada's only Olympic medal in ice dance—and three bronze medals at the World Championships. Several ISU members have since told Wilson that they should have been first at Calgary, especially in the free dance.

Wilson was there when McCall got the news that he had contracted AIDS. If you knew Rob, you can clearly hear his voice in Tracy's description of their three-way exchange with the doctor. So many of us had similarly heard Rob playfully stretching the truth—as his partner warmly admonished—in conversations under far less grave circumstances.

The metaphor in her last sentence says it all.

I remember it so well. We were on tour and he hadn't been feeling that well. He was saying he was having trouble getting into the programs, and I could hear when he was lifting me that he was really grunting and struggling, so I was teasing him about it. We had about two weeks left in the Stars on Ice Canadian tour, and he called to say that he didn't think he could make it because he was feeling really sick. I had to go on tour anyway because of all the group numbers. That was totally out of character for him. I realized he'd never ever missed anything. He always skated through things.

I was talking to Brian [Orser] one night and he said that a friend said Rob had lost a lot of weight. So I said, "You don't think it's AIDS, do you?" Brian said he didn't. Then we were joining the Boitano–Witt tour and Rob said he felt he was strong enough to come and do it.

You try and say, "Okay, it'll be all right." You've got these fears, but you keep pushing them down. It had been two weeks since I'd seen Rob and we were meeting in the Toronto airport to join the Boitano–Witt tour.

And then I saw him.

Total shock. This was not the Rob I knew and loved. Two weeks, and [the change] was so dramatic. He was gray, and he had lost 20, 30 pounds. He'd lost everything. There was no life in him.

He was, "Hi, how ya doin'? You look great, blah, blah, blah." I ran to the bathroom and sat there to compose myself, because he wasn't dealing with it. He was just, "Everything is wonderful."

I came back out, then said, "Gotta go make a phone call," to regain my composure. It was like treading on eggshells. I didn't want to hurt him, but I knew something had to be done.

I said to him, "Look, you've gotta see a doctor...just to make sure...you don't want to push it." He saw the doctor and he said, "There's no problem. [I should] just take it gently."

So we kept working, and the day before the show was the dress rehearsal in Portland, Maine, and he knew that he had to skate it out more than he had been doing in practice. And he just started to hyperventilate. He collapsed on the ice. Barb Underhill said, "Tracy, we have to get him to the hospital."

In the hospital, they were asking him questions.

"Have you been sick for very long?"

"Oh, about a week."

I said, "He's been sick for five or six weeks. He's been having trouble breathing."

"Have you been on any medication?"

"Oh, no, no, I was on antibiotics for a week."

I said, "He's been on antibiotics for four weeks."

He was like a child. You just wanted to take care of him. He was maintaining that everything was going to be fine.

The head doctor came in and said, "Who are you? You family?" I said, "No, I'm his partner." He said, "Out!"

We were in emergency, so there was a curtain around his bed. I went outside the curtain and heard the doctor say, "We got the X-rays...and it looks like you have the pneumonia associated with AIDS."

I went into the waiting room and I just remember the pain in my stomach. What a way for him to find out. He was so childlike with the doctor. It was just, "Oh! Okay. All right." I didn't know what to do. I walked around in a circle, and remember looking at the pay phone on the wall and saying, "Who do I call?" I went in to see Rob once the doctor left and he said, "Well, the doctors think it's pneumonia…the pneumonia that might be associated with AIDS. They'll do tests and we'll have to wait and see." He kept being kind of chipper, but surprised.

I said I'd go to the rink and tell them we couldn't do the dress rehearsal. That was a big thing for Rob. "I'm going to be here a couple of more days," he said, "so tell them we can't do the rehearsal today. A couple of more days. We'll probably have to meet the tour a little bit later."

When I got back to the arena, they were practicing the opening number. They would announce the name and the spotlight would go on the performer.

I walked into the rink. There was a spotlight on the ice and the announcer said, "Tracy Wilson and Rob McCall."

And then the light went out.

KRISTY SARGEANT

The Gift of a New Life

At the elite level of figure skating, there haven't been too many competitors who could look up into the audience and wave to their five-year-old daughter. But when Kristy Sargeant, then just 23 herself, completed her pairs free skate at the 1997 Canadian nationals, that's exactly what she could do.

Sargeant and her partner, Kris Wirtz, finished sixth at Worlds in 1997, their best ranking ever. But there was a time, six years earlier, that Sargeant thought her career—and life as she had known it—was over. Single motherhood, especially teenaged single motherhood, is not the norm for figure skaters. And it's not warmly embraced by the skating world. Already nervous and confused, Sargeant felt coldly rejected by a skating community that had been her home since she herself was a little girl.

But, with the help of her family and her live-in partner, Wirtz, Sargeant has prevailed. She concedes that there have been rocky moments, that in the early days she obviously wasn't mature enough to handle the responsibility.

Now, though, she wouldn't have things any other way.

When I found out, I thought it was the end of the world. I was 17. Young. Very young. Actually, when I found out, I was at an international competition at St. Gervais-Oberstdorf. I was skating pairs [with Colin Ehms]. I was five months pregnant when [the news] all came out…and I was still skating. I thought it was the end of the world. I thought, "Oh, my God, everyone's going to hate me. They're going to call me names." Which they did. But I mean, that's people.

It was very scary for the first, probably, month. And then, after that…well, my family was really supportive, and I said to myself, "You know, this isn't going to be the end of the world. It's going to be the start of a new…of a new life."

I had Triston, and one month later I turned 18. It was hard because it was almost as if everyone deserted me…all my friends, my coach, everyone. The papers were cutting me up. It was really bad. Saying stuff like, "Her partner dreamed of this and she let him down." One story was right under a Mark Messier story. Everyone saw it. It was saying mean things. It was really painful, plus the father wasn't really too involved. And his family wasn't really too supportive…actually, telling me to give the child up for adoption. I didn't consider that. Not at all.

Then after she was born I kind of went through a wild stage. You know, 18. I didn't know what was going to go on. So when [the call came], I thought it was a start to a new life. Paul [Wirtz] phoned me in Edmonton, where I was doing singles. He said, "Do you want to come to Montreal for a tryout?" Without a word of a lie it took me two seconds. "Sure I'll come." And then afterward, I kind of said, what am I doing? I have this life here. I have a daughter. I have everything here. I don't know if I should do this. I talked to my parents and they were very supportive. Two days later I flew to Montreal to train with Kris.

I had been living with my parents, and they took care of Triston. It was very hard for me because Triston was my whole life and then I had to leave her. But I think in the long run, it really turned out for the best. She's with us now. You come home and have no energy and you're tired, and she's full of energy because they have naps at school. So that's hard. But without her I don't know what I'd do.

I really find I'm a lot more mature because of what I've gone through and what Triston brings to me.

Right from the beginning, Kris and I started living together. He has been really great. Will we have children together? Maybe, but not for a long time.

JOHN NICKS

The Crash

John Nicks won a World Championship in pairs in 1953 while skating for Great Britain, but he is more widely known for what he's done with American skaters since 1961.

On February 15 of that year, the first crash of a commercial Boeing 707 killed all 18 members of the United States figure skating team. The accident occurred near Brussels as the team was on its way to the 1961 Worlds in Prague, which were then immediately canceled.

Also killed were eight of America's top coaches. Nicks was one of the coaches that the USFSA petitioned to come to the States to fill the void. Another was Carlo Fassi, and a few others arrived in ensuing years.

By the 1966 Worlds in Davos, Switzerland, the Americans had reascended. They took a bronze in men's, a silver and bronze in ice dance, a bronze in pairs and a gold in ladies, thanks to Peggy Fleming. It was a remarkable recovery. Fleming was coached by Fassi at the time, but she had also been trained by Nicks for a year. Nicks has taught, as well, Ken Shelley, Robert Wagenhoffer, Christopher Bowman, Tiffany Chin and the current world-class pair Meno and Sand.

It was a very unfortunate happening for U.S. skating, that crash, and I, fortunately, was able to get the coaching position in Southern California. I replaced one of the Olympic coaches, Bill Kipp, who was killed in the crash. I think Carlo Fassi, who went to Colorado Springs, was the only other European who was brought in at that point.

Colonel Stork, a U.S. judge who judged me when I was skating, was, I think, the secretary of the USFSA at that point, and he contacted me and said, "Come on down to California." I was in Canada in a little town called Trail [British Columbia]. The Trail Smoke Eaters won the World Hockey Championship when I was there. It toughened me up. I was the only figure skating coach in town...and it was not really a figure skating community. I can remember standing in the middle of the rink, trying to avoid being knocked down by hockey skaters, who'd heard I was a "fancy skating" coach. It was very good for me because Southern California was very competitive, too.

I remember sitting in the living room, watching television, and the shot of the crash site came on and I could hardly believe it. Information was a little vague in those days, but it soon became apparent that everybody had been killed, including all the team, a lot of parents, a lot of officials, I think about seven or eight coaches. I was just appalled, and so sad because I knew many of them.

Then I got the communication from Colonel Stork—who I'm sure communicated with a lot of coaches—asking me if I'd like to go down to the United States to work. And I did, because my work in Canada in those days was seasonal. I was married and I had two children and I really was looking for 12-months-a-year work. I was very fortunate. A tragedy for others worked out well for me.

How quickly American skating rebounded amazed me then. It doesn't amaze me now. I know American skating now, and with all due respect to the rest of the world, I don't think there's one country that has the depth of skating the United States has. The volume.

The American nationals is a wonderful competition. Nobody, absolutely nobody, is safe. This year [1997] they had two champions dethroned who were both excellent. And the year before, Todd Eldredge lost.

The Europeans probably think we're crazy.

FRANK CARROLL

No One to Call

Everyone in skating remembers where he or she was when hearing about the 1961 airplane crash over Belgium that killed the entire American team. Frank Carroll, one of the world's foremost coaches, remembers it well. Sometimes too well.

I was actually offered the job John Nicks took at Paramount, but I was in Ice Follies, performing. They wanted me to leave the show and fill that position after the crash.

I lost everybody. I lost my coach, Maribel Vinson Owen. I lost my best friends. I lived at Maribel's house. Both her daughters were killed, Laurence and little Maribel. My best friends were all killed. I was from Worcester when Boston was the hub of skating. There was Bradley Lord, Gregory Kelly,

Maribel Vinson, Laurence, Maribel Jr., Dudley Richards. There was Gregory Kelly's sister.

They were all on that plane.

I had turned pro and Maribel was supposed to go to my opening. She was flying out of New York to Worlds, and my opening for Ice Follies was at Boston Garden and she told me, "I'll either be flying to the Worlds or I'll be at the opening, so look for me. If I'm not there, you'll know I'm on the plane."

So I did the show. I knew she wasn't there, and that night the phone rang after the opening…and she was dead.

I still start to cry when I talk about it. You know, it wasn't until years later that the real sadness set in. When you're young and you're a star in a show and a great tragedy happens, it's very sensational. Everyone wants to interview you, and everyone is holding everyone and it's all sensational, you know what I mean?

But the deep pain and the deep sorrow don't come till years later. When Linda Fratianne was competing and her rockers pointed wrong in school figures, I couldn't pick up the phone and call Maribel and say, "Maribel, I can't fix her left inner rocker—it's pointing crazy." [Maribel] was dead. And I started to cry one day, because the person who'd taught me everything—my philosophy of life, my philosophy of teaching, all my technical knowledge—wasn't there for me. There was no one to rely on. I had to figure it out myself.

It was years later that I really understood this.

ROBIN COUSINS

The Great Carlo Fassi

It was one legend passing on to another the bad news about a third legend.

"Have you heard?" Dick Button asked as he came into Robin Cousins's broadcast booth.

And Cousins knew that Carlo Fassi was dead. He was aware the great U.S.-based coach had been taken to the hospital in grave condition a few hours earlier after collapsing in a lounge at the arena in Lausanne during morning practices of the 1997 World Championships.

Fassi's life was celebrated in a memorial service at the International Olympic

Museum a few days later, but his death cast a pall over the week of skating. He was a giant in this sport, a creator of champions. He had coached Peggy Fleming to an Olympic title, and Robin Cousins, and Dorothy Hamill.

I spoke with Fassi the day before he died and he talked about how thrilled he was with the progress Nicole Bobek had made now that she had returned to being coached by him and his wife, Christa. He was sitting in the hotel lobby so that his cigar smoke did not fill up their room. We promised we would talk, for this book, later in the week. Later never came.

Robin Cousins was a 17-year-old with lots of potential but not enough career direction, when he won the European bronze medal in 1977. His coach, Gladys Hogg—"who taught John Nicks how to skate"—only traveled by car or train, and the ensuing World Championships were in Tokyo, so Cousins would not have a coach. Carlo and Christa Fassi agreed to look after him there.

"He came to me," Cousins recalled. "The great Carlo Fassi! I always thought you went on bended knee and asked, 'May I be honored?'"

A knee injury stopped Cousins right in the middle of his free skate, but he liked the way Fassi handled the situation, and agreed to spend the summer studying under him in Colorado.

That summer turned into three years and an Olympic championship.

The whole point about going to somebody like Carlo is this. I've always said there are a lot of people who know how to cut diamonds, but there are very few who know how to polish them in order to put them in a museum or put them in front of people who go, "Aren't they beautiful?"

That's what he did. He had this uncanny ability to be able to focus people, to be able to polish them and make them look great, without making them look the same. Carlo could take on five or six—and when I was with him nine or 10—national champions at different levels and never create anything that resembled a rivalry or a jealousy or a resentment. It was absolutely just through honesty and an across-the-board situation. Everybody who worked with him trusted him 150 percent or didn't work with him at all.

I thought, "This is somebody who believes in what I want, believes I have the capabilities of doing it and will do his damnedest to help me do that. And if at the end of the day it doesn't work out, it isn't because I didn't have the good coaching or didn't have something else. It was just one of those things." You would never stop and think, "Well, I wonder what if?" There were no what-ifs with Carlo and Christa. And that was what made it so special for me to work with them.

Coming from a situation where my training was weekly what my competitors' was daily, and suddenly being in a position where you don't have to skate if you don't want to because there's ice later; there was as much of a trust from his point of view to the student as there was the other way around. He would offer his opinion, whether you wanted it or not, and if you didn't take it, then it was your problem.

An example of his trust. In 1980 in Dortmund, [Jan] Hoffmann came off the ice and Carlo immediately in his mind calculated, looked at me as I was about to step on the ice for my long program and said, "It's over. You can't win. Not possible. Go have fun." And I did. It was the best skate of my life. I had nothing to risk. It was an exhibition. I threw in an extra triple. I was through the roof. I didn't have time to consider the consequences of not winning. Either he knew, or it was just instinct, to say it's over, just go have fun. Because he knew that at the bottom of my heart I hated to skate for the judges. I've always said my motto is "Skate for the audience because they're the ones who have paid." That allowed me to go out with a bang.

We have lost a lot of friends in this sport recently, but this one. . . . Christa said to me, "But where else should he have gone?" An actor wants it to be onstage and a movie star wants it to be in movies. For him to have been in his element at a World Championship—doing what only Carlo Fassi could do, which is be passionate about the sport, 150 percent—was the only way.

SUSAN HUMPHREYS

A Higher Power

Figure skating does not seem to have as many born-again Christians as do other sports, particularly football and baseball. One explanation could be that it's a sport of younger people, who have yet to go through certain life crises.

Susan Humphreys became a born-again Christian in 1995, and says she knows of only five others in skating: Paul Wylie, Danielle and Stephen Carr, JoJo Starbuck and David Liu.

Humphreys won her first Canadian title in 1997, after finishing third three times and second once. That second-place finish put her on the 1994 World and Olympic teams, and after a terrible 26th at Olympics, she moved up to ninth at Worlds and seemed to be the logical successor to Josée Chouinard as the next Canadian hope. But she began experiencing serious back problems in 1994, then ran into conflict with her coach, Christy Ness, over the handling of the injuries. They parted company—"She didn't want to coach me anymore"—and Humphreys endured a rough couple of years competitively, before recovering in 1997.

Her faith was put to the test at the 1997 Worlds, however, when the skin around the "skater's calluses" on her ankle became seriously infected. She struggled through the short program, then spent the night in a Lausanne hospital. She was forced to withdraw from the next day's free skate, and landed in the hospital again the following night.

A t first, when I was having highs and lows in my career, I wasn't a Christian. The 1993 national championship was a real high for me, and it went higher for me in 1994, when I was second. And the Olympics were a high and a low at the same time. I was so happy to be at Lillehammer, so excited to be there. It was one false moment of whatever it was—lack of focus, fatigue—that set in for that silly double Lutz, that seemed small at the time but that changed my life in a lot of ways. I fell on the Lutz, which was ridiculous—I've been doing double Lutz since I was seven years old. So I didn't qualify for the free skate and I was devastated, because for me at that time I didn't have any perspective on anything. It felt over. I felt really sorry for myself.

Then, that year at Worlds, I came back and I was really strong. I was ninth, and from such low confidence I just fought back.

Then the real injury and coaching things started happening. And within that next year was when I became a Christian. I always say that faith found me—I didn't go looking for it. I just saw things in such a different way. No more of this "Why do I feel sorry for myself?" "Why doesn't this happen for me?" I'm strong enough to handle it, and maybe this is a compliment from the higher power. He knows you can deal with it, so He's giving it to you, because you're the one who can handle the job. Just as you're the one to be the woman to represent Canada.

I had been invited to see a sports speaker. I didn't even think twice that it was in a church. It was just one of those moments that literally brought me out of my chair and to the front to give my life to Christ. It was a very odd moment, and at first I didn't really know what to do with it. And that's often the case, because there's really no one to guide you.

Now I've got a lot more knowledge. I'm involved with a lot more friends who are Christians. My brother is, actually. He had become one the year before when he'd been on a hockey trip in the States. We didn't even know that each of us was.

You start to see things that have a lot more linking. That's why when all those things went a lot more haywire for me—the injury with the back and the coaching problems—I just really feel that those things are meant to be, and that's the way you see it when you view things the way I do.

Then I just went through the next couple of years with my skating, rebuilding for the next thing, realizing that was where I was given my ability and that's where I should be. I've always believed in use it or lose it, because not everybody has it and you have to recognize your ability and where it comes from.

At Canadians, I went through that last-minute self-doubt. I would say [to God], "Put me where You need me." When I was at [1997] Canadians, I just felt sick. You know when it's there for you. I knew that it was now or never, because the next year, to go in having not won again, would have been really hard for me. There was this little church right across from the hotel . . . of course. I walked in and just sat there at the front, lit a few candles and wrote in the prayer book, and when I walked out of there I just had this overwhelming sense of "It's going to be all right." I don't pray to win. I pray for me to be a strong person and to put me in the place where You need me.

When things didn't go well for me at Worlds, although it was hard at the time and you feel a bit for sorry for yourself, all of a sudden I said, "This is where you're supposed to be and you've gotta just sit on it."

That doesn't mean you don't try your best or that you don't try to be better the next time. You're given only so much, and you have to use it. It's not going to just happen for you.

CRAIG SHEPHERD

Life Imitates Art

In 1991, a movie called The Cutting Edge *did decent business at the box office. Starring Moira Kelly and D. B. Sweeney, it is about a pairs skater and a hockey player who join forces in a successful pairs partnership.*

In Skate, *a 1996 book, I wrote that the premise was "a huge stretch if the viewer is familiar with figure skating or hockey and their almost contradictory skating styles." Right in theory, wrong in practice.*

I hadn't counted upon the determination of a young American hockey player named Craig Shepherd and his Russian wife, Natalia Mishkuteniok. That would be the same Mishkuteniok whose extraordinarily flexible pairs spins helped her and Artur Dmitriev strike gold in the 1992 Olympics and 1991 and 1992 World Championships, and silver in the 1994 Games.

Since stepping on the ice together for the first time on April 1, 1996, Shepherd and Mishkuteniok have worked diligently to become a pairs team, hoping to score a berth in a tour or be invited to a professional competition. They get up at 2:30 A.M. to drive to a rink where they can get free practice ice at 4:30. Then Shepherd has to report to his day job as a strength and fitness consultant.

They've been working with renowned coaches Uschi Keszler and Tatiana Tarasova.

If it all sounds a lot like The Cutting Edge, *it should.*

That's why we started this. It was the middle of January and we were watching the movie. I had the movie in my video library, but Natalia had never seen it. As we watched, we looked at each other and started laughing. And the next day we went into the rehabilitation center where I work. I learned how to do a star lift off the ice. The lifts were really easy because I'm strong, but I had no technique at all. I'm six-two, 200 pounds, so I could lift her. I just bulled her up there. Put my hand here. Put my hand there. Lift.

Then we decided to give it two months to see if it would work or not. So I got my skates from Harlick, and I ordered my blades. I had to learn to skate all over again. We went to Indianapolis to work with the man who taught me how to skate for hockey when I was a kid. His name's Pieter Kollen and he went to the Worlds in pairs back in the 1960s. Out of all the people we've worked with, he had the hardest job of anyone. I looked like King Kong or Godzilla out there.

Those boots hurt so bad compared with hockey skates. They're so stiff. It's a whole different ballgame. I'm a hockey player, first off, psychologically. I'm skating in front of figure skaters, a lot of whom don't think hockey players can skate anyway. And here I am out there proving that fact because my feet hurt so bad, and I'm in these skates that have toe picks on them. And I know a lot of these people are saying, "Yup, there's the hockey player . . . he skates like one." It was so frustrating. Finally my boots broke in and things got a lot better.

To date, and I should knock on wood, I've tripped on my toe picks only four times. Which is really good, I think. I don't think about them anymore.

The balance point is totally different in figure skating. You're back on your heels more. I've got Gold Seal blades, which are supposed to be rockered blades, but they're nowhere near what a hockey blade is, rocker-wise. Figure skates are much flatter and the blades are much longer.

For me it was a lot more fun to go backward, at first, instead of forward, because I didn't have to worry about the toe pick.

I was a skater when I played hockey. That was my game. And I think the biggest misconception is that hockey players can't skate because they're not doing Axels. But think of a guy going to the net. He's got a 230-pound Uwe Kruppe on his back, hooking him, slashing him, trying to bring him down. And then he comes in on Patrick Roy and he's got enough balance to keep Uwe Kruppe off of him, deke out Patrick Roy, score a goal and not kill himself, all at the same time. That's unbelievable skating skill, but people don't see it that way. I think it's a misconception from the past that all hockey players do is fight.

Natalia doesn't want to go out on hockey skates. She says she'll fall down and kill herself because the blades are totally different.

I just hate it that neither of the sports respects the other. It's so stupid. Both sports can learn from each other. But it's always the hockey player saying, "Aw, that guy's a fruitcake," and the figure skater going, "Aw, that guy can't skate." It's been this ongoing war for many years and it's stupid.

As far as we're concerned, we've surpassed any goals that we've set for ourselves. We were hoping to have a nice little, maybe two-minute, program where I could go out and do a lift, maybe a death spiral, maybe a throw, and not look stupid while I was doing it. We thought if we did that in the first year, we'd really be cooking. In the long term, skate in a show, maybe.

We worked with Tatiana Tarasova—she was the one who gave us the program—but it was all by phone, and she sent us a videotape of a couple she had skating the program, from the Russian All-Stars tour. She thought it would be good for us because I'm playing a Mongolian. I do very strong movements—I don't have to look like Baryshnikov on ice. It uses a lot of Natalia's flexibility and my strength. We got her bent up like a pretzel in this program.

We finally got to work with Tarasova in person in March of 1997 and we were at her apartment with Ilia Kulik and Oksana Grischuk, and Tarasova told us that this program, and we as a team, were ready to compete professionally.

And I just about fell off the couch.

I've been talking to Tom Collins, to IMG [International Management Group], and it seems everyone we talk to is very curious about what it's going to look like, but I don't think anyone believes that it's for real.

The problem we're facing is that no one—outside of Uschi and Tarasova—believes it.

TODD ELDREDGE

A Kind Kind of Place

Although he has won World and national championships, Todd Eldredge is one of the most down-to-earth people in any sport. You get some sense of why when he tells you about his hometown.

If you look at a map of Cape Cod, you'll see that Chatham, Massachusetts, is right on the elbow. It's the kind of place where people make a living from the sea, the kind of place where you're not going to grow up with a swelled head.

And it's the kind of place where, when they find out the local kid might have to quit his sport because it's getting too expensive, well, they all kind of just pitch in.

You know, I really don't know how big Chatham is. It's a small town, a couple of thousand people, maybe. I'd say back in 1985, my parents were having a little trouble paying for skating. I was living away from home in Philadelphia—it was just before moving to Colorado—and it was getting harder and harder to finance it. Some people in the town found out about it and decided, "Well, let's see what we can do. Let's try and get a fund-raiser going and see how much money we can raise."

Every year they would have a Christmas dance, and they would also have a summer clambake where people would donate their time and efforts to put the event on. People would pledge however much they wanted to. It was a whole group of people who organized it.

I was able to go to a couple of them. They used one of the hotels that's right on the water as kind of a beach house. They'd set up a huge grill out in the back and they'd cook whatever you wanted. Everyone donated the seafood and that was fantastic. People loved that. They got a chance to go in and sit down and talk with everybody. There were a couple of tourists, but it was mostly the townspeople. It was a chance to get together and it was for a good cause. It was for something they were hoping would be successful one day . . . and finally it was.

They did it from 1985 up until the 1994 season. They were going to do it only until 1992, but they said, "Okay, another Olympics is only two years away, so we'll do it for another two years."

Then after 1994, with all the changes in the sport, I can make so much money now that I don't need that support anymore.

My dad is a commercial fisherman and my mom is a private-duty nurse—she goes to people's homes and takes care of them. Providing the weather cooperates, my dad goes out every day. He gets up at the crack of dawn and he's out on the water long before anyone else is even awake. He puts in a long day. He's done by four o'clock every day, but he's up at four in the morning. He'll go 20, 30 miles offshore and catch different varieties of fish. I've been out with him a couple of times, but not that far offshore. I've kind of been in the bay.

I'm tremendously thankful. I don't really know how long I could have gone with my parents supporting me. You never know. I'm so happy they did something like this, and it's given me the opportunity to take my career as far as I have.

STEVEN COUSINS

The Three Tenures

Everyone knows, or should know, by now that Steven Cousins is not related to Robin Cousins. Strangely, though, Steven's parents are from Bristol, which is also Robin Cousins's hometown. And Steven's first competitive victory was in Bristol, with Robin presenting the trophy!

Great Britain is trying to improve its developmental system, but outside of dance, it has produced skating stars only in rare and isolated bursts. John Curry and Robin Cousins winning consecutive Olympic Games was an anomaly. No British man has won a medal at even the European Championships since Robin Cousins in 1980. But Steven Cousins came close, finishing fourth in 1995.

Steven Cousins, whose eight British Championship titles is one more than Curry amassed, is a charismatic skater. Only inconsistency of performance and the lack of a triple Axel have kept him from pushing into the top five in the world. When he became the first Briton to land the Axel—in combination with a double toe loop at the 1994 Olympics—he seemed destined for the World podium. It has not yet happened, and his best finish at the event was his eighth place in 1995.

He is one of the most popular skaters with his peers, and can shed some light on skating in three different countries.

I started skating just by chance. We live in a really small area about 25 minutes away from Manchester, just over the border in Wales. There is only one recreational thing to do and that is play football [soccer]. So I used to play soccer all the time. Two houses down were some friends of ours whose kids were going, "I can skate and you can't, na-na-na-na-na"—that kind of thing. So I tried it and hated it. I left it, but my older brother Paul carried on and he was really good, just took to the ice naturally. After about six, seven months I got jealous-brother syndrome. So I tried it again, and this time took to it a bit better and kept going from there.

The coach we had was pretty relaxed, but we really looked up to her. [She was] a great coach and more of a friend. When I was 10, her husband got a job way down the other end of the country. She decided she'd come up three days a week and teach us. After the first week, she never came back. We're still waiting for her to tell us that she's not going to teach us anymore.

Donna Gately had just finished touring with Holiday on Ice, and my dad went over to meet her and see if she was interested in taking the job. We hit it off right away and I stayed with her for eight years, the biggest portion of my career. I became primary champion, and the same year I won the junior championship and went to Junior Worlds.

When I was 18, I had a really rough time at the Munich World Championships [1991]. One of the team leaders, who shall remain nameless, had a good go at me in the team meeting. I was destroyed by it. And then it hit the press. It basically was just a nasty scene. Donna, I think, was just blown away by the kind of pressure I was being put under. She felt she had taken me as far as she could, and I should go away and train somewhere else. I felt gutted at the time. I couldn't understand why. Now I realize she's probably the most unselfish person I've come across. Just mind-boggling.

It went from bad to worse. I went to train in the States with Mr. [Alex] McGowan. It was an interesting time. I was always a fun-loving character. And when I got to Sun Valley, it totally changed my life and I still deal with it now.

It's a beautiful place and the people were so supportive of me. But Sun Valley was a temporary job and Alex McGowan was trying to find a permanent job, so we moved to San Francisco, which is when things started going wrong. I had a great home life because I was living with the Yamaguchis. Fabulous people. So good to me. But things were getting progressively worse on the ice .

I had a pretty good Olympic experience at Albertville, but the next year, Worlds at Prague, was when I just couldn't handle it anymore. Let's just say that if I wanted to go to the bathroom, I had to ask [the coach]. I'd lost all my friends and couldn't understand why. No one would come up and speak to me for more than five minutes for fear that he would come up. It was really hard to find a sense of myself, and sometimes I'm still struggling to find that. The straw that broke the camel's back was an evening practice in Prague. I was just wiped, but I had to do the practice and it was just awful. I couldn't sleep that night and went to ask if I could go for a walk, and he said, "No, stay in your room." Just like that. Peter Jensen [the sport psychologist] said that for me to stay in my room all day, all I would need is a rope and I would take care of myself. That is not me. I have to be doing things. So that is basically what killed it.

In my mind, I was going to quit. I didn't want to skate anymore. It was just not fun. A friend of mine, Jan-Erik Digernes from Norway, called and told me to meet him at the Eiffel Tower, and we bummed around Paris for a week.

He said before I quit I should try Mariposa. I called Doug [Leigh] and he said, "We'd love to have you," and a couple of days later I got a call from Elvis— "Hear you're thinking of coming. You should." And I figured out it wasn't the sport that I didn't like...it was the environment. I took two weeks in Canada to see how I liked it. Absolutely loved it, and haven't looked back since.

The three countries are very different in skating. In Britain, it's totally recreational. The athletes are the business people, the association the amateurs. In the States, everyone is a businessman. Everyone. And [skating is] run like a business. You're a commodity. But I find there's a lot of support there. It's a win–win situation. If you win, it makes everyone look good. And when you're up there, they help you. They let you stay there. They don't try to knock you down a peg the way they would in Britain. In Canada, I find there's a perfect balance between the two. It's work hard, play hard. The support I receive from the Canadian association is second to none, and it's not even my association. In personal style, I'd say in Britain everyone works to survive. In the States, you have to work to get money so you can get somewhere. In Canada, everyone works so they can enjoy life.

KYOKO INA

A Family Tradition

Kyoko Ina started skating pairs with Jason Dungjen in 1991, and by 1997 they had won the U.S. Championship and been to four Worlds together.

But Ina was a pretty experienced skater by the time she joined the partnership, having competed internationally for Japan in singles. Her father was born in Japan and her mother was born in Washington, of Japanese parents. Kyoko herself was born in Tokyo, but moved with her parents to New York at the age of six months. That still left her eligible to skate for Japan.

My whole family on my mother's side competed for Japan, so it was sort of a family tradition. My mother was a swimmer on the national team. She never made the Worlds or Olympics, but she won the Asian Games. My grandfather was a long-distance track runner and he was at the 1924 Olympics. And my grandmother played tennis at Wimbledon.

So it was sort of like, "Why is Kyoko going to represent the United States, when everybody else has represented Japan?"

When I was 14, my coach and parents convinced me to compete for Japan. They said it was for family reasons and it was also to get a lot of exposure. The depth of skating was not as great as it was in the United States at that time.

Midori Ito was a senior at the time and I was a junior. Yuka Sato was the big name in juniors. I pulled out just before senior nationals [in 1988], so I never got a chance to compete against Midori. She and I were pretty good friends, and that was one thing I would really have enjoyed—competing against her.

I pulled out because I didn't want to fly to Japan anymore. I was 14, 15 and 16 then. All my friends in the States were competing at local competitions and at regionals and qualifyings. I'd be training with them and all of a sudden they'd all disappear and go to a competition. And I was still at home training. My friends were here. So it was fairly difficult to leave them and go to another country. And even though I had friends there, it just wasn't the same.

Within the three months of the competition season, I'd fly over to Japan four or five times. I was really young, so jet lag didn't really kick in, but it was just really hard. I was away from my school friends. I was away from skating friends. It was just a really hard time. Everyone's rebelling at that age anyway.

I competed at Junior Worlds for Japan. It was a gamble to come back, but either I was going skate for the United States or I was going to quit skating. Fortunately, it turned out well.

Everyone was very supportive. They knew that I skated because I loved to skate and at the time [that I went to Japan], it didn't matter where I skated. But I eventually realized it wasn't what I wanted. I pulled out the day before I was supposed to get on the plane for Japanese nationals. I was crying, not because I was upset that I'd pulled out, but because I didn't want to go. If they had put me on the plane, I would have been really angry. My coach and parents asked me why, and I said either I wasn't going to skate anymore or I was going to skate with my friends. My coach was kind of surprised that I said that, but everyone was very supportive.

The next year, I won junior nationals in the States. Jessie Mills had just won Junior Worlds that December, before nationals in February, so she was the favorite to win junior nationals. So for me, it was a big accomplishment.

[Skating for the U.S.] was a very good decision for me. It didn't matter if I won nationals, I was just so much happier.

INGO STEUER

No Money, Better Parties

When the Berlin Wall fell in 1989, Ingo Steuer was 23 years old. So he'd spent nearly a decade in the famous, or infamous, East German sports training system.

The adjustment to Western practices hasn't always been easy for athletes who grew up in the far more regimented east bloc regime.

Steuer and Mandy Wötzel, with whom he won the 1997 World Pairs Championship, serve in the German army reserve for three months a year, living in a barracks, taking military training and then driving four hours on the weekend to practice. They're in a special company comprising athletes of all sports, and are expected to remain in the army until after the Nagano Olympics.

Wötzel is six and a half years younger than Steuer, but she, too, has memories of "the old way." She recalls that when she was young, she bought an ice cream cone one afternoon—skaters were supposed to watch their weight and diet—and the next morning the coach knew not only that she'd eaten the ice cream, but what flavor it was.

Steuer doesn't miss that kind of scrutiny, but it had one small social advantage: the feeling of getting away with something made the parties a lot more fun.

It was the 1983 World Junior Championships and I was on the podium, and I watched the East German flag and they were playing the national anthem. And this was great.

One year after the Wall fell, I heard the national anthem of Germany when I was on the podium...and it was very different. Before it was the East German and the West German. The first time with just one [Germany] it was very difficult, I felt the East German anthem was great for me. The West German anthem was not me. But now it's the same.

The other system in East Germany—it was a good system for sport. If you were good in sport, you could go wherever you wanted...Japan, West Germany and the States, anywhere. And you got old? What the other people in East Germany didn't get—fruit, bananas—you could get. Now it's there, but then it was not. My feeling is that this system was good for sport because we had a lot of time for practice. We didn't pay for this—it was all the government. And we had good coaches.

Now it's different. We have not-so-good coaches overall in Germany, only a few, and the best coaches come from East Germany. We have had the luck to have the sports education from East Germany and we can carry it forth. But in East Germany, we didn't get money, and now we can get money. I think the money we used to get from touring went to the government. It was the same as Russia or Czechoslovakia, all over the East.

When we went outside of East Germany, it was difficult. We never went anywhere alone. We went, always, two or three or four people together, and maybe one person in the background—I don't know who it was. In that time, it was dangerous to have a party with the other guys, the other sportsmen, after the competition. But we had, every competition, a party. Nobody knew this and we had a lot of fun. After the Wall fell, [having a party] was legal, and we had not so much fun. When the Wall fell, my birthday was a few days later and we had celebrations for both.

I was happy with the way I was treated [in East Germany]. The sport was good. The life we had back then? It's much better now, because now we can make money skating. In East Germany when you finished with figure skating you could get work. You finish now or you're injured...you have nothing. But now while you are skating, you can have money.

ILIA KULIK, ANJELIKA KRYLOVA, OLEG OVSIANNIKOV, IRINA LOBACHEVA

In America, We Don't Have Such Problems

Although all skating champions have always been partly defined by the country they represent, the athletes and coaches have always treated international borders lightly. It's a practice that goes back to the middle of the last century, when the Father of Freestyling, Jackson Haines, fled America for acceptance in Europe. Sonja Henie did the opposite, because the U.S. was where the money was. American Brian Boitano was choreographed by a Canadian; his Canadian rival Brian Orser was choreographed by an American from Germany. Countless Europeans have trained in North America, and Americans and

Canadians have sought coaching in Europe.

But that phenomenon always stopped dead in its tracks at the border of the then Soviet Union. Soviet skaters trained and lived in the Soviet Union. Period.

When the Soviet empire collapsed, skaters and coaches began emigrating: to Western Europe, to Israel, to the East, to North America. They sought better facilities and better economic opportunities. And a better social and political climate. The 1997 gangland-style murder of Valentin Sych, president of the Russian Ice Hockey Federation, underscored the dangerous anarchy that percolates beneath the surface of the post-Soviet sporting world. High-profile athletes have become the target of robberies and extortion.

Ilia Kulik, silver medalist at the 1996 Worlds and European champion the previous year at age 17, switched coaches before the 1997 season, leaving Victor Kudriavtsev in Moscow and switching to Tatiana Tarasova, who had moved to the New England Sports Center in Marlborough, Massachusetts.

Anjelika Krylova and Oleg Ovsiannikov, ice dancing silver medalists in 1996 and 1997, followed their coach, Natalia Linichuk, and her husband, Gennadi Karponosov, to the University of Delaware. At first they shared a house with other Russians living there, but then they moved into their own apartment. They both say they're often homesick for Moscow.

Irina Lobacheva and Ilia Averbukh, a married ice dancing couple, decided to remain in Moscow after Linichuk left for America in 1994. But after dropping a couple of spots at Worlds (from 13th to 15th), they, too, moved to Newark, Delaware. They leaped to sixth in 1996, before slipping to seventh in 1997.

In general, Russian athletes do not like to talk at length about what is happening in their native land. But they all agree that, for the time being, their situations are better on this side of the Atlantic. The ease with which they can get from home to their training site is the one facet of American skating life that seems to most impress all four.

Ilia Kulik

The facilities are great. We have four ice rinks, a gym and everything. Fresh air. It takes me only five minutes to get to the rink.

And I have a new hobby now—I shoot pistols on the shooting range.

When I switched coaches, we didn't have enough ice. Victor had lots of ice.

Tatiana didn't have ice in Moscow, which is another reason I moved.

I had some problems with conditions in Moscow. Not very good ice. I always have ice, [but] sometimes it's not prepared. Sometimes it's cold. Sometimes it's very cold. There's no gym. No place for choreography. I have to do this in the hall, and it's not very comfortable.

I do a triple Axel on the floor. I've tried to do a quad Axel on the floor. It's a Russian tradition to do the jumps on the floor. I've done it since I was seven.

The traffic is very bad in Moscow. And life in Moscow is a bit dangerous now. If you lived in Moscow you'd know. When you go out, you don't know, maybe somebody put a knife in your stomach.

No one has tried to take money from me like from the hockey players… maybe I don't have enough money.

Oleg Ovsiannikov

We don't go up to see the other Russians in [Simsbury] Connecticut during the season because it is a two-hour drive to New York, then two more hours to where they are. So four hours just one way. And we have only one day off in each week—Saturday. And, of course, we sleep that day.

In the summertime, we may go to New York for fun, but in the season we don't have time. When we do have time, we sleep. The second practice of the day finishes at 12:30 midnight and the first practice starts at nine o'clock in the morning. We practice from nine to twelve both times, in the morning and at night. In between we do some ballet off the ice.

And I play Sony Play Station. A lot.

Anjelika Krylova

We have an apartment. We have a car. We have ice. The first year it was very hard, really. But now it's the same. We miss home, of course, but we have a lot in the United States. Now it's much easier. And when we go to competitions we have some friends there. My mom is now in America, and she feels very good to be here.

We don't meet the other Russians who are here. We just practice, practice. We don't have time.

Irina Lobacheva

In Russia we have a lot of problems. In our training, for example, or to eat, to get fast food, for example, and many other such problems. In America we don't have such problems, of course. We eat more fast food than in Russia.

In America it is more comfortable for us. It is a small village where we live, and it is quick to get to the rink. Maybe three minutes. We can concentrate on training. In Moscow, it's a very large city, and you have traffic and it takes a long time to get to the rink. It takes maybe one hour to reach the ice rink by car.

We have money in America, but not enough. We don't have any sponsors, but we get prize money from skating. The Russian Federation gives money, but only maybe $30 a month. In Russia many people have the same.

It is not much.

ELVIS STOJKO

A Way of Thinking

Focus. The word is so overused, both as noun and verb, in all sports that it has lost its meaning. But when you see it, really see it, in action, you understand why athletes so often refer to it. If there was a more complete word, they would use it. But there is not.

The men's short program at the 1997 World Championships was one of the greatest evenings for depth-of-field performance in skating history. Four men— Alexei Urmanov, Todd Eldredge, Ilia Kulik and Elvis Stojko—were fabulous: state-of-the-art athletic prowess and absorbing presentation. It was nearly impossible to choose among them, but the judges had to. And when they did, Stojko stood fourth. That meant even by winning the free skate, he could not win the gold without the trio above him rearranging themselves.

The Stojko camp was incensed. Their guy was two-time World champion, had just won the Grand Prix Final two weeks earlier and should have had the judging momentum, they thought. You could feel the white heat of their anger as they talked. A little too calmly, a little too in control, it seemed. But what was really going on was a marshaling of emotion. Drawing anger in, to be transformed into something that could be useful in the free-skate final.

And Stojko came out and landed the quad–triple in the free skate, and simply blew the field away—although Todd Eldredge skated wonderfully, to finish second. There had been a lot of possible distractions: the death of Carlo Fassi, the news that Scott Hamilton had cancer, Stojko's own situation after the short. But Stojko did not allow any of this into his head.

Stojko's unparalleled ability to focus comes partly from his training in the martial arts, which uses a Zen-like approach to thinking.

The following thoughts were spoken a few weeks before Worlds, but they capture the process that went on at Lausanne.

It's a matter of being able to control what your mind is doing. And that is the hardest thing—the conscious effort to make sure you're in control. Your body always follows your mind. Your mind is the control center, and if you can control that, you can control everything. It's a lot easier said than done, as most people know.

In 1996, I just had trouble trying to focus in. There're always times when you'll say, "I had trouble focusing today. Physically, I was fine—mentally, I just couldn't focus." That's going to happen sometimes.

To be honest with you, during the 1996 season I was up and down. At times I really focused and at times, for some reason, it just wouldn't click in.

Focus can also be attributed to change. There is a change physically when you're growing up. At 17 and 18 years old, I gained 20 pounds and strength and more power, and I had to deal with that. You're becoming a more mature person. You're understanding more things. Things aren't as small as you thought they were. There's a more open perception, a bigger picture.

And mentally you develop. What you've done might be a negative—not winning the World Championship, for example—but [because of] what I gained from the experience, I'm glad [it] happened. Because I learned so much from it, mentally, and was able to pass it on to experience.

What is the head space of martial arts? It's hard to put the human mind into words, the pictures you have and how you go about it. But if I was to mention one key point that makes a difference, it's to be able to know yourself.

To pick yourself apart mentally, to watch yourself interacting with other people. Being in isolation teaches you nothing. But to be able to interact with people in a stressful situation, in a confrontation, and *then* from that point sit back and analyze, reflect on what you've done and then understand how you reacted, then control that reaction—that's important.

Being able to face your weaknesses is a big thing. I've always tried to make sure I do. I've been doing that since I was a kid. It's a hard thing to do. Some people can't face that—"Oh, I'm wrong here. I'm wrong there." A lot of things I've cleared up—a lot of things that people say, "This thing could be a negative." I see part of myself having different attributes that are negatives, but for what I do they are positives, in order to get where I want to go. It's that hungry attitude, where, say, moto-crossers or guys who race F-1s have to be aggressive. They might have to be a jerk when they're out there in order to be the best, to be aggressive. People will shun them for being that way, but they have to have that attitude or they're not going to make it.

And it's just knowing yourself, being independent and being open with yourself and then reflecting on who you are.

MARINA ZOUEVA

All Painful, Still Now

The death of Sergei Grinkov on November 20, 1995, struck a chord whose amplitude could not have been predicted. The traveling friends who are Stars on Ice were devastated and so was the larger skating world, and that was to be expected. But the degree to which his death affected the North American public at large was stunning. His youth, his vigor, his young wife, his baby daughter, Gordeeva and Grinkov's two Olympics and four World Championships, their painfully exquisite final amateur program when they returned from the pros, the purity of their style, their assimilation into the North American professional circuit as the most recognizable Russian skaters ever—these factors all played roles in the outpouring of grief and support directed from the American public to his tiny widow, Ekaterina Gordeeva.

Grinkov's death, in a much less sinister and far more limited way, had a little of the Kennedy to it. A legend felled in his prime. His shocked and frantic wife with him as he died. Camelot destroyed in a few seconds. For it was obvious to even the most distant of outsiders that Gordeeva and Grinkov were, and probably always had been, in love. Unconditionally. You just had to watch them skate. Their eyes never left each other. And it was the same off the ice.

One of their closest friends was choreographer Marina Zoueva, who was on the ice at Moscow's Red Army Club with them in 1982 when the two first teamed up. She was also on the ice with them at Lake Placid, New York, in 1995, for their last minutes together.

Zoueva immigrated to Canada after G and G turned pro following the Goodwill Games in 1990. She had been a world-class skater herself, finishing fifth in Worlds with her ice dance partner, Andrei Vitman, before retiring and returning to school to study ballet and coaching.

She still becomes emotional when she talks about Sergei Grinkov, who was a friend and role model to her own son, Fedor Andreev. "They would come to my house or I would come to them," she says. "I know it won't happen, but I keep having the feeling he will come in again."

While describing that November morning in Lake Placid, Zoueva had to pause a few times to regain her composure. Although she speaks fluent English, the emotional intensity of the discussion sometimes drew her back into a Russian accentuation and structuring of her sentences. We have left it that way to carry the full impact of her memories.

I started to work with Katia and Sergei in 1982, when Katia was 11 and Sergei 15. I did their choreography. I just did their program. I can't tell now, but they were so looking good, and they were very coachable. It was very easy to work with them and I would enjoy a lot. The first program was not very much choreography. We did a lot just on working for parallel movement and correct positioning. It was not art at all.

I never saw before so pretty, the two of them, so, so talented.

We got very close. We had so many practices in other cities for competitions, and lots of time we spent together. Every month we stayed in the same hotel, have the same schedule, take the same bus, go to the same movie, even store. All spent together.

They were really friendly from the beginning. They never fight or say something bad to each other. It was very, very natural always. For me, now looking back, it looks like it should happen, their love, but I couldn't tell you at the time. Katia was changing a lot. She was a little, little girl, girl, girl. But one day

I saw, "Oh, this is not a kid anymore. This is a young lady." Sergei probably saw that, too. They were very close from the beginning and respected each other.

I didn't see them at all for maybe one year. They come to Ottawa with Stars on Ice. It was 1992, I'm sure, because Katia was pregnant. And she tell me, "Marina, I make the baby," and I was so happy. After her baby they came to me again and they decided to go back [to Olympic skating]. I had a lot for them, the music and design, because in my mind and my brain I saved everything for them.

I did their solo for them in May [1995], but it needed work. They asked me to come to Lake Placid before the performance [set for later in the week]. We made the music Grieg's Piano Concerto, the adagio, the middle part. We had everything, but we had not created their last positions. So I came to Lake Placid the day before, and we did this, and changed a little bit the elements. We had a great evening together.

It was Monday, about 11 in the morning.

In Grieg's adagio from the piano concerto, it is the best of the romantic music. Everyone who writes history of music says it is the best of romantic era of music. It starts with little tears, and in the middle the whole orchestra starts to play very loud music. That was very much for Katia and Sergei. This music was special. They had a throw double Axel. After the woman has landed the man should accelerate a little bit to get closer to her.

He started accelerating and then stopped.

He stopped, and he skated around the rink from the right side to the left side, keeping a right direction. And Katia skates toward him and says, "Sergei, what's happening?" But he not tells her anything. He wasn't really conscious.

It was the famous music playing. The perfect music. It was where the orchestra plays...the full sound. Right at that moment. If you listen to Grieg, you will know what time that happened. In the music, when it comes full.

He very, very gentle lay down. The left hand touch ice and lay down. Squeeze a little bit. I run because I can see something wrong, but I think it's his back. He had a lot pain before. I ran [toward the other rink] and I said, "Somebody, fast!" Nobody follow me and I said, "Katia, go again." But doctor come very soon, very soon. When got I back, I touch him. He had no pulse and his face was a blue color. I was not scared at all. When we take CPR course, the lecturer said it should be very quick. If no pulse, doctor come and everything. I just think about that. I start and then doctor come. They start with oxygen and everything.

Katia and I sat together because Katia didn't know what was happened. She don't understand at all. So I just explained to her. It's hard believe what happened. For everybody. She lived Sergei—well, her whole life I can say—and he never said about heart something. Never. Never.

Sergei was so healthy and he so much loved life. Some people is always something wrong, and not enthusiastic for life.

I couldn't believe for a long time that this happened. I could not believe.

I did the tribute [program] not for Katia. I did for Sergei. It's all painful when I think about Sergei. All painful, still now.

I think if she wants to skate, she should skate. I was sure she can be a good singles skater, too. I know even before—I can make a right program for her for sure. I was not scared. Sometimes when you start work with somebody, you think it will be good or not. But with Katia, no. I was sure it will be good and well done.

When Katia skates everyone, anyway at least now, thinks about Sergei when she comes on ice. And that makes sense, because Katia, she looks great and beautiful, the same like it was in the pair. Alone, but same quality, same level... you understand what I mean. Even maybe a little bit better because she was his partner and she was his great wife and now in her place, it's like he's still there.

It affected a lot of people. First of all, they were so perfect, and they have a great image. When they skate it was so sensitive for everybody. Also, people lose dreams and they were like a dream for everyone. Great skaters. Great career. Looking good, and nice family, beautiful child. It's not happen very often in the life if you look around.

Everything was absolutely amazing. And when is broke, one moment, one day, all people have shock.

TOLLER CRANSTON

An Olympic Champion's Hand

Everyone has strong memories of Sergei Grinkov. This is Toller's.

With Sergei and Katerina I had a very special relationship, but I wasn't their best friend. I had commentated about them, I had judged them, I had choreographed for them and I had skated with them.

In Symphony on Ice, for four shows in 1995, we always had the part where, for some reason, he and I were partnered at the very end, and he had to hold my hand in this big lineup of the stars and we had to run to the other end of the ice and do a little choreography.

It was during this time that he would grab my hand quite aggressively—it was never the other way around. I didn't really want to take the initiative because I wasn't sure if he liked me. In an intellectual way, I had the sense of being Ekaterina Gordeeva—what it was like to be partnered by Sergei and what it would be like to skate in the Olympics holding that hand, because that was your partner.

It was a very comfortable hand to be held by. It was a very big hand, strong hand, and kind of a fleshy hand. Sometimes when you shake hands with people your hand doesn't fit or it's uncomfortable, but for that duration of the 10 steps we would have at the end—and Ekaterina was on his other hand—I always deep down inside had the sensation of being his partner.

And it was in some strange way very credible. Just by touching that hand, I kind of felt Olympic greatness. I felt that's probably why they were so great—because of the energy coming out of that hand. Maybe if I'd been holding her hand, I'd have felt the same way.

He used to, in some strange way, enjoy correcting me about those silly little choreographic steps. For some reason he took pleasure, in a kind of avuncular way, of correcting somebody much older. Because that was his duty—he had to look after me, he had to hold my hand, he had to drag me across the ice and he had to correct my steps.

I've never discussed this before, [but] I always enjoyed the experience, I was always touched by it and I was always kind of awed by it.

And I had it and experienced it. No one now can ever experience it, because he's dead. I had that little intimate—at least for me—experience with him that left an impression on me that I cannot forget.

EKATERINA GORDEEVA

Skating Alone

One of the most stirring moments in skating history occurred not in competition, but during a special performance of a touring show. On February 27, 1996, in front of a sold-out audience at the Hartford Civic Center, Katia Gordeeva, stepped out onto the ice.

Alone, for the first time.

It was Stars On Ice, "A Celebration of a Life," a tribute to her late husband, Sergei Grinkov. For Gordeeva the performance, designed for her by Marina Zoueva, was an important part of the grieving process and—although she wasn't sure about it at the time—the first step of her solo career. She rejoined Stars on Ice later that spring for the company's tour through Hawaii, Japan and Korea.

For the 1996–97 season she returned to Stars, skating solos and group numbers. She also competed in a number of pro competitions, winning a silver medal in the U.S. Professional Championships in November.

That same month, her book, My Sergei, *appeared. It was cowritten by the gifted* Sports Illustrated *writer Ed Swift. The idea first came to them when Swift was interviewing Gordeeva for an article in the program for the Hartford show.*

My Sergei *is a runaway success, constantly in the top five on every bestseller list since its release. It touched a nerve across an entire continent because it is exactly what its subtitle calls it:* A Love Story.

I definitely was surprised at how well the book sold. I wasn't sure how it would go. I thought, "This story is really too simple. It's nothing special I was saying in the book." But after I'd done the book, I realized that this is the point—that there is really nothing very special. It's just a story that everyone can understand and relate to their own life. The simplicity, probably.

I have to say that Edward helped me so much. He was so understanding to me. There was no language barrier or anything. He brought a lot of books. He wanted to know every place we went in Russia, everything interesting, how to spell every single word.

It was difficult, definitely difficult, in the very beginning. When I was done with the story, when I was done telling everything to Ed, I thought I probably was never going to be speaking about it again. It was work. I understand now that you have to go through the hard time, the most difficult time, to get something good.

First of all, I'm very happy that I'm skating with Stars on Ice again, and seeing all my friends every day. They help me a lot. They just bring me back alive. I'm really feeling well now. I'm really happy that Daria is around me often.

I'm glad that I can skate. I know that my single skating will never be even close to how we skated together. I cannot feel off the ice the way I do on the ice. All the emotions and all the feelings I can bring on the ice helps me a lot. How to explain. Something I feel when I'm skating that helps me to satisfy myself with living, that I can do something, really, for people. That I can do something in real life.

I was surprised when I came back [to skating] and I got so many notes and so many people were supportive with phone calls, with gifts for Daria. And how many people were interested. It felt like all of the United States was interested in my story. And we were Russians—we weren't even Americans. But they were so close to my story, so interested and supportive. I didn't get that much support in Russia even, from just regular people.

I don't think very much ahead. But I'm going to try and compete again. I did five competitions in 1996. I didn't plan it—it just came up. Oksana Baiul was pulled from one competition and they said that maybe I can go. It was very difficult, but my first competition was a team competition, so it was very comfortable. I had my team, the Russian team, competing with the American team and Canadian team, so I didn't feel really like I'm lonely. And then my Marina Zoueva was supporting me and then Galina Zmievskaya was helping me in some competitions and it just brought me confidence. And then every competition I see my friends. But the last time I had a competition in singles was maybe when I was 10 or 11 in Russia.

I'm trying to understand what I'm doing on the ice now, and I feel quite confident. I'm really looking forward to trying different styles in skating, and just improve myself, maybe with the jumps. Maybe I'll try some rock and roll, because I never really did it. But I don't have clear plans what I'm going to do.

My mom helps me all the time with Daria. She travels with me when I need Daria around. I'm very lucky, actually.

Stars on Ice is a kind of family because we've been together for such a long time. We travel together for four months a year. I know everyone much better than I know maybe even my sister. We know how difficult it is to travel, especially if you're alone, especially if you don't have family with you. It's so difficult and we try to support each other, try to somehow make each other feel happy today. I don't feel like really, really family, like "This is my father" or "This is my sister," but definitely best friends, and I'm really happy that I have it.

People like Scott Hamilton, Kurt Browning, Kristi Yamaguchi—those are people who can make good atmosphere around them. Especially with what happened with me. They went through this difficult time with me. They were the people who were with me all the time. They were at Sergei's funeral. They supported me after. I think for the whole of my life they will stay with me as my closest friends. Even a lot of my relatives weren't so close to me during this time as they were.

I am optimistic about life now. It was very hard for the first year. Every month changed. After a year passed, it's getting better and better.

Marina knows me since 10 years old. She knows me so well and I know her because me and Sergei were her first pairs skaters, her first team. So we kind of grew up together, she as a choreographer and we as skaters. She definitely knows me better than I do, as a skater.

I always admired ladies' singles because I couldn't even imagine how to go on the ice alone, go through the program alone, not holding someone or not feeling support. Not feeling that huge arm around you that will take care of you.

Which is why I was so scared, the first time, because right from the beginning I started to skate pairs and I've never been alone. And here are a million people looking at you and you just have to go and skate.

Am I proud of myself? Yes, I would say so. Maybe I'm not at that point where I will be really, really proud of myself, but I'm still very glad that things go on and that I can compete and skate.

Relationships

TRACY WILSON

Why Haven't I Been Skating?

We will never know what great works of art were left unskated because of Rob McCall's death in November of 1991. We do know that the body of work that he and Tracy Wilson assembled, first as amateurs and later as touring pros, was— outside of Torvill and Dean's—unrivaled in their era for its depth and breadth of theme and artistry.

Wilson and McCall were the prototype of the opposites-attract theory of partnerships: they were different in so many ways. Yet they were of one mind in the most critical areas. They were committed to creating a higher plane of ice dancing; they recognized and embraced that their opposing temperaments created an uncommon chemistry; they respected each other's polar-opposite lifestyle; they were extraordinarily hard workers; they shared a keen sense of humor and an understanding of people; and they cared about each other deeply . . . loved each other. Like a married couple, they would often finish each other's sentences, especially if the sentence happened to be a particularly wry observation on the state of the world.

Tracy Wilson is fulfilled by her marriage, her children and her career as a skating commentator. But she also senses the tiny tug of something missing. How could there not be, after you go cheek-to-cheek with a friend a few hours nearly every day for a decade . . . and then he's gone?

Something's really hit me in the last few months. And it involves my kids, because they started to skate. My five-year-old loves skating. He loves more the hockey side, and I've been out there on the ice just playing. And it's the first time since Rob got sick that I've gone out on the ice and played.

I was out with my son on the outdoor rink. We were just playing around, and there were all kinds of kids on the ice, and I thought, "Gosh, this feels so good!" And I realized it was because I was skating.

I started thinking back. "Why haven't I been skating?" I skated eight hours a day for most of my life. I was more comfortable in my skates than in my running shoes.

I think that what happened was, when Rob got sick all my thoughts went to him and skating was just too painful. So I never did it.

And I realize now that I grieved for Rob, and still am, and never gave my skating career a second thought. There was a wall there. When I get out on the ice, it's just so apparent that Rob's not there. Still. And for me to go out and skate—I still don't feel comfortable with my left hand because there's nobody holding it.

In ice dance, everything you do is with that person. You don't skate alone. So to all of a sudden go out there and skate—Rob not being there is totally apparent.

So what it told me was, I guess, is that I've got a lot I still have to deal with. I've been able to keep involved with skating and with my friends and all of that side, but the actual loss of skating personally, I have to deal with. I know it's painful and that's why I haven't done it.

I do miss him in my day-to-day life. His humor. Rob always had another way of looking at things. I miss that and I miss the fact that my kids won't get to know him.

I skated until I was 29, and there was nothing that I loved more than skating, and I think [its absence] is something in my life that I'm going to have to go through.

I don't go out and skate at all. The number of people who kept asking me, "Don't you miss it? Don't you miss it?" And I didn't give it much thought except [to say] "No. I have a new life." And I guess that was just the quickest answer. But in reality I couldn't get past missing Rob to even allow myself to think about the skating. It was as though he was the focus. And I think I'm getting close to the point now where I need to get back on the ice and skate and get used to the feeling of skating without him.

JAYNE TORVILL

The Royal Couple

Watching the interaction between Jayne Torvill and Christopher Dean and the thirsty British press corps during the pair's unparalleled reign as World ice dance champions was like watching a royal couple under siege by the paparazzi. Distant, formal hand waves; quick, innocuous comments from the principals; the apologetic but hasty exit. The British media had fallen head over heels for fantasyland relationships in the early 1980s, when Torvill and Dean won—and "won" grossly understates their dominance—four World titles and the 1984 Olympic gold. Prince Charles and Lady Di were at the peak of their popularity, and the horde of British writers who followed Torvill and Dean wanted to cast the skaters in the same mold. It was overwhelming to the shy couple from Nottingham as the mobs descended upon them at every opportunity, hoping for even a word or two. Story after story was printed, speculating that Torvill and Dean would do the obvious and get married—a second idealistic regal wedding for the public to feast upon.

But Torvill and Dean were not romantically involved. They were, in fact, great friends and partners in the most creative tandem in figure skating history. It's difficult, if not impossible, to find anyone in skating who does not feel that they are the greatest ice dancers of all time.

And, unlike the other British royal couple, their partnership has survived. Through several stages. They took their first steps together in 1975 and, almost without interruption, have had full, active seasons every year since then. If they weren't in training for amateur competitions, they were rehearsing or performing one of their groundbreaking professional tours. They drew full houses all over the world, even attracting months of sellouts in Australia, where figure skating had been barely more than a distant rumor.

Ten years after their Olympic triumph with Bolero—one of the top three skates in history—Torvill and Dean returned to the amateur ranks when pros were reinstated for the Lillehammer Games. They finished third, with many observers coming away thinking that they should have won. In the three weeks prior to the Olympics, they had battled illness and completely revamped their program. Disturbed by the reaction to their free skate at the Europeans, they discarded 80 percent of the material and rebuilt the routine in time for Lillehammer—an absolutely impossible task unless you've been together 20 years, have a back catalog of superior moves upon which to draw and know exactly what makes the other person, and your partnership, tick.

Lately, they've taken a different approach. They're headliners with Stars on Ice, and don't have to carry the whole load of audience expectation. Oh, yes, and although both partners eventually did get married, it was not to each other.

The hope that Jayne Torvill expresses in the final sentence here? No worry about that: they brought much more than "something" to this sport.

I never had any thought that it would turn out as big as it has. I had been doing pairs, and when I didn't have a partner anymore, I did singles for about a year. But I wasn't going anywhere with that. I was kind of too old for the standard I was at. Then, when the opportunity came along to dance again, I thought, "Great." I really had no idea how far we would get. I just liked doing it.

We just took each thing as it came along. And after all of it, when we turned professional, our dream was to get one of our own shows. We never thought that we'd still be skating now. We thought, "Maybe five years," as professionals. Then, of course, as we kept going and going, then came around the chance to do Olympics again and we thought we'd take that chance. Following that we had a chance to do another big tour, and after 1994 the professional competitions took off and we had a chance to do more of those.

At first, when the press started to really follow us and speculate that we'd get married, it was hard for us because we were so sort of innocent and naive about the whole thing. We couldn't believe people would be interested in our personal lives. We thought they should only be watching us skate. We used to get very embarrassed about it. As we get older, we get more cynical and sarcastic about it. We think it's funny now.

We both have the same goals, but we achieve them in different ways. We both enjoy the creativity. We enjoy doing something new. We enjoy performing. After all these years, we're in sync when we're working together. Choreographing, we kind of know what the other's thinking. If we're just starting to choreograph something, we keep playing the music over and over. Sometimes we stop the music and go off and do a whole sequence of steps that fit exactly to the music because it's in our heads already. Then we put the music back on and it works, because we've got the rhythm in our heads.

Sometimes Chris will explain something and I'll say, "I don't think it will work that way. We'll have to do it this way," and we'll go ahead and try it. We know instantly if something's going to work, because we've done sort of variations on it in the past. We can visualize it, too—whether it's worth pursuing, if it's going to look nice or not.

When we're taking a break and we're going to skate individually, it's funny. After, like, 10 minutes I get really bored because there's no one to do anything with.

He has a more aggressive nature. Everything has to be done quickly and now. I sort of sit back and do things thoroughly. We get to the same place at the same time, but in different ways. He might be able to see something quicker than I can...but I get there eventually.

He really used to be terribly shy. I used to be less shy than he was. I wouldn't say outgoing, just less shy than him. Now he's much more confident in himself. When he was younger he was more insecure. I think for guys doing skating, they're very aware of comments—"It's for sissies," and things like that. So they play [skating] down a lot. But as you get older and you achieve more success, everybody thinks you're wonderful and they don't worry about [it so much].

I think we'll carry on for a couple of more years, while we still can. I think we appreciate it more now because we know we haven't got that much longer to maintain this standard and this level. So we're really enjoying it.

We've had stages. They've all been progressive. The miserable times have come when we've had to miss something through injury, which has not been often, considering the number of performances we've done over the years. We've been lucky, really.

We're never satisfied with what we're doing. We always think we can do it a little better. I think that's probably what's kept us going. We're very critical about our work. We discuss other people—"We like this" or "We don't like that"—but we're hardest on ourselves.

If we can be remembered for bringing something to this sport, then I think that's great.

CRAIG SHEPHERD

Two Continents, One Love

Craig Shepherd is an American who decided to go to Russia on impulse. Natalia Mishkuteniok is a Russian who decided to come to America to learn English.

He was a hockey player, she a figure skater.

Paths that should never have crossed? Possibly. But fate had other ideas. And now they're married and skating together in America.

Mishkuteniok was the 1992 Olympic pairs champion with Artur Dmitriev, and Shepherd grew up a hockey player in Edina, Minnesota. He played college at Michigan State, and spent time in minor pro hockey before going to Europe to play. While watching the European Championships in Düsseldorf, Germany, he was taken by the skating and shooting ability of the Moscow Dynamo team and thought he'd like to try it, although only one other North American had ever played in the Russian Elite League. He studied Russian at home for a couple of months and joined Dynamo, where he, the goalie and the Russian doctor were the only people who spoke English.

He was introduced to someone else who could speak English: Natalia Mishkuteniok.

I met Natalia over in Moscow and then we lost each other... it's like the Doctor Zhivago thing. It was a freak that we ever found each other again. We dated each other there secretly. Nobody knew about it. She didn't want everyone to know about it... I guess because I was American. She'd had people write things about her before that weren't true. There was an article in an American magazine, for instance, that said she was married, and she wasn't married. So we didn't tell anybody.

But we lost contact with each other. She was going to show me around Moscow before I came home at the end of our hockey season, but I had to leave early because the war in Chechnya was going on. When I left, she had moved apartments and I couldn't find her, so we totally lost touch with each other.

She comes to New York to go to New York University and is studying English, right? I have no idea where she is. A friend of hers here in Colorado Springs—Irina Vorobieva, who's a coach—says to her, "There's a new strength and conditioning coach here in Colorado Springs. Do you want to come and work with him and we can see each other again?" She never told Natalia my name, and Natalia said, "Sure, see if he has time for me." Now Irina comes to me and says, "Craig, there's a pairs skater who's an Olympic gold medalist, a pairs skater who's a friend of mine, living in New York, who's coming here. Her name's Natalia Mishkuteniok. Do you have time to work with her?"

And I'm sitting there going, "No way!"

Natalia didn't know it was me. I went to Irina's house and picked her up. When I opened the door it was a *huuuuge* surprise. We were married two months later [December 1995].

And we're still going strong.

SHAE-LYNN BOURNE

The Best of Both Worlds

They have been compared to Torvill and Dean in the innovative approach that they bring to ice dancing. And like Torvill and Dean, the man is a career ice dancer, while the woman started in pairs. Also like Torvill and Dean, Shae-Lynn Bourne and Victor Kraatz have always recognized the nature of their relationship. They are skating partners, comrades in creativity, extremely close friends. They are not romantically involved.

Since reaching the podium at the world level in 1996, the couple have had their sights squarely set on a World and an Olympic title. Much of that will depend, of course, upon ice dancing's politics.

When you're nearing the top of the skating mountain, skating is more than a full-time job; it's a preoccupation. Especially when it's pairs or dancing, because you are not dealing with just your own needs and psyche. The partnership requires attention off the ice as well as on it.

So if you're going to maintain an outside relationship, you accept that it will be a challenge. Especially if it's long distance. Shae-Lynn Bourne, a Canadian skater training in Lake Placid, New York, dates Steven Cousins, a British skater training north of Toronto, but doesn't find it a problem.

Actually, I don't believe at all that it's difficult. I think it's a very easy thing to have a long-distance relationship if there's love involved. If it's true love, it's an easy thing to deal with.

In a lot of ways I think it's a better thing because you become better friends. I know with my relationships, most of them are built on friendship first, just really knowing the person. I'm always talking on the phone. I really get to know the person, and you understand each other. So when you do get to see each other, it's so special because you want to take advantage of every minute that you're together. I've noticed that with my boyfriend, and with my mother, my sister and my brothers. When I do get home, it's the best thing because I don't waste a second when I'm with them. I think some people who are together all the time get used to it, and they start realizing their differences and they start getting irritated with each another. When I have that time, I use it, and I enjoy it.

Same with being with Victor. It's like a marriage in many ways because we're spending all our time together on the ice, and a lot of the time off the ice we have to spend together, thinking about what we want to accomplish. Because we're different, we have to compromise. You really learn to understand a person and how you have to deal with them. I've grown a lot by skating with Victor.

I've never questioned if Victor and I would stay together or not. I just knew we would. I knew when we first stepped on the ice we would always be together. I felt right away he was my perfect match on the ice.

It was funny when we first got together, because he has a European background and I always assumed that in dance, Europeans have to get married. That was my understanding. I was 15 when I met Victor and I said to my mother the first day, "I'll skate with him, but I'm not going to marry him. Just so you know that."

We have different backgrounds and [come from] different cultures and that's how we're different, not because of him being in dance and me being in pairs. But that's really balanced us out and we've learned to understand each other and how to deal with each other on the ice and off the ice.

I was very young when I started with Victor. I was 15 and he was 20, so he really watched me develop. I think all along I've never looked at Victor deeper than being a partner or a brother. To me he was more a brother figure than anything. That's how I looked up to him. I think that's just how our relationship has developed. It never hit that point where we thought of love. It was just the love of skating in our relationship.

When I was younger I said I'd never want to date a skater because in my mind that would be the worst. But as soon as I dated a skater, it was the best. Because we understand each other. We understand what it is we do. We can support each other when we're down or when we're up, and we really understand the sport. It wouldn't be the same with an outsider. I couldn't imagine seeing anyone outside of skating, because I don't think he would have the same understanding of the sport, the dedication it takes. Steven is away from home, too, so he understands that side of it and he just has a great perspective on skating and life. I wouldn't be where I am if it wasn't for him.

Steven has been incredible. He's only been encouraging about Victor. He and Victor are great friends. Steven is a people person. I don't think he has an enemy, to be honest with you.

I get the best of both worlds. When I'm out there with Victor, he's my best skating match. Apart from skating, Steven is my perfect person match.

JEAN-MICHEL BOMBARDIER

Good Atmosphere, Good Skating

Relating to other people sometimes has as much to do with what's going on around you as it does with what's going on between you. The right ambience can bring out hidden strengths; the wrong one can magnify insecurities.

Jean-Michel Bombardier is the first to admit that he has lacked consistency, and sometimes confidence, during his career. He and his partner, Michelle Menzies, won the Canadian Pairs Championships in 1995 and 1996, but those titles were sandwiched between two disappointing finishes: a seventh and a third.

Bombardier is married to Josée Chouinard, a former Canadian champion, and admits that it's difficult to maintain two important relationships at the same time. But it's a lot easier when you're feeling confident in yourself and your work, and comfortable with your surroundings.

I'm a guy who had the potential to do three Olympics, and so far I haven't done one. It's not exactly a nightmare, but for some reason I was never able to perform in Olympic year.

It's been up and down all along for me. It was especially down in 1992, after being eighth at Worlds in 1991 and then missing my first chance at the Olympic team.

In 1992, I was skating with Stacey Ball and she really changed a lot body-wise that year. It was to be expected, but you never want to face it. We got out there and didn't perform the way we had in the past few years—that fall we had won Skate Canada. There was potential to go to the Olympics, even though physically we didn't match anymore. But we finished fifth. And Michelle was fourth with Kevin Wheeler, for the fourth year in a row, and you needed to be third to make the Olympic team.

So, I changed partners after that and went with Michelle. It was actually during the Olympics that we tried out. The big goal was the 1994 Olympics and we had two years to get ready.

Everything was going pretty well, but we didn't know each other. Everything was focused on the training. And that did go well. We were second at Canadians and seventh at Worlds that year, so expectations were really high the next year.

The way we were trained in Montreal we didn't get to know each other at all, so we were fighting all along in 1994 and we had a hard time to get along. We had some injuries to deal with, too. After being seventh at Worlds, we were seventh at Canadians. We were fourth in the short program and I was totally finished. There was no way I was going to pull up, for some reason. I don't know why I was like that. I was just mentally not ready. We were in a good position to make the Olympic team, but I just did not get my stuff together at all.

It's not a ranking that I'm very proud of, but the next year we came back strong—switched coaches and won the nationals quite easily. We took a break after 1994 and we didn't know what to do, stop skating or whatever. For a few months we didn't skate together, and the only reason we came back was that in April you are committed to club shows and carnivals. We weren't getting any lessons from any coaches and we started to get along better. We were skating well at shows and we said, "We're not finished. We can do better."

That's when we decided to move to a new coach and a new atmosphere. Our relationship improved, but we had to work at it, because the seventh place at nationals really destroyed our confidence in ourselves and each other. We changed that by going to a positive atmosphere, which Mariposa is. You go there and there are all those top people, led by Elvis. And it just worked for me. Doug Leigh is very positive when he coaches singles and Lee Barkell is about my age...he's just a bit older than me. I wanted somebody who would respect me and I'd respect. I wasn't a kid anymore.

I could be with Josée more, because she had left Montreal the year before. I feel much better. I feel that at the same time I'm skating, I have something outside of skating. We're building something, Josée and I, and I have skating to make my living.

It's not always easy. Sometimes I'll say, "It's okay, because I have something else in my life," and that's not fair to Michelle. So I really have to respect that when I'm at the rink, I put 100 percent into my skating...and when I get home I just leave my skating at the rink. I try to separate the two people... because it's tough to have relationships with two women at the same time. But one is my work partner—the other is my life partner.

Our first year at Mariposa turned into probably the best year we've had since we skated together, for consistency. And that's one of the problems Michelle and I have—consistency. We can skate really well in practice, but in competition it's not always there. Except at Worlds. At Worlds we always show up and skate well.

When we won the Canadian title [in 1995] after what we'd gone through, it was hard to believe. It was a relief to prove yourself. It gave us a lot of confidence in our personality. And the way they present you when you go somewhere, as a Canadian champion—it's always there. No one can take it away from you. Even in 1997, when we finished third, we were upset, but I'd had a lot of problems with my equipment, so being third was okay. It was the year before Olympics and I was, "Okay, it's fine. Next year I'll be all right and it's Olympic year." And our relationship is strong enough for that. We have more confidence.

It's the third opportunity for Olympics, and I don't want to miss it.

JENNI MENO AND TODD SAND

A Normal Relationship Off-Ice

While most pairs or dance couples who are also linked off the ice started their skating relationship first, Jenni Meno and Todd Sand were the opposite. They were each with other partners—Jenni with Scott Wendland and Todd with Natasha Kuchiki—when they became enamored with each other during the 1992 Olympics in Albertville. By that summer, they were going out together and had formed their pairs team. Keeping with the Olympic theme, they became engaged during the Lillehammer Games, in which they finished fifth, and were married in the summer of 1995. They have such a rapport that their coach, John Nicks, says he sometimes feels like an intruder during practice sessions.

Sand told CTV researchers that their personalities mesh well: he's laid-back and levelheaded; she's outgoing and aggressive. Meno says that the romance "helps with handling the pressure. We're there for each other all the time."

That theory was put strongly to the test at the end of the 1997 competitive season. After a steadily climbing career that included three straight national titles, two World bronze medals constructed upon elegant, under-pressure free skates and a successful 1996 fall schedule that included a victory at NHK and silver at Lalique, Meno and Sand ran into three straight disappointments within six weeks. First they lost their national title to Kyoko Ina and Jason Dungjen when they were off their game in both programs; then they had to withdraw halfway through the Grand Prix Final because of Sand's back problems; and then they dropped two spots at Worlds to fifth.

Jenni Meno

When we started together we also started dating each other. So from the beginning we always had the two relationships that we had to separate. So it wasn't like something that was a big change for us.

We've always tried to separate the two. Usually if we have a problem on the ice, which all pairs do, by the time we leave the rink it's finished.

Skating is skating, and you have to have another life, too. Sometimes we have to make a conscious effort to do other things and remember, "Okay, let's just forget about skating and let's go out to dinner and go to a movie and do something else." We really try to do that and have a normal relationship off the ice.

I think on the ice [being married] is a benefit to us because we are so close we almost know what the other person's thinking, and so we can really relate. Sometimes, I guess we can be pickier with each other than with someone else. I don't know if that's good or bad.

You don't want to bring personal life onto the ice. I think maturity has something to do with that. Some young kids 13 or 14 years old, if they had some sort of relationship and they were skating together it might be much more difficult.

Todd Sand

I think experience has something to do with it. We were both singles skaters before we even started skating pairs, and we learned how to compromise.

When we're working on the ice, we both know why we're out there. We love to skate. And we know we want to be as good as we possibly can be together as a team.

So once we're done skating we don't take that off the ice. I mean, we know that the reason she wanted my finger held "like that" was that she wants me to be a better skater…and not that I didn't do the dishes. We're not really too worried about that.

ISABELLE BRASSEUR

Skaters Understand Skaters

In August of 1996, Isabelle Brasseur and Rocky Marval were married in a bilingual ceremony in Montreal. In attendance were Lloyd Eisler and Calla Urbanski, who had more than a passing interest. Eisler is Brasseur's pairs partner and Urbanski is Marval's pairs partner.

Brasseur and Eisler were four-time Canadian champions, twice Olympic bronze medalists and 1993 World champions. Urbanski and Marval, who had dissolved and reassembled their partnership a couple of times, were American champions in 1992 and 1993, and reached seventh at the Worlds. Both partnerships are now in professional ranks.

There have been a few occasions—a tour in Brazil, Elvis Stojko's fall tour through Canada—when the two pairs teams have traveled together. And occasionally on the pro circuit, as in their amateur careers, they'll face each other competitively. It's a tough situation for husband and wife, but it's also the source of a few jokes—about fraternizing with the enemy, for example.

But, generally, when they're skating it's in different places—not a particularly ideal arrangement.

I t's not always easy. I guess in a way it makes it exciting because you're gone and then you're together, you're gone and then you're together, and you have something to look forward to.

But it's really hard sometimes, because even though we're both in the same circle, often we do separate things. If one of us has the weekend off, often the other one works, and obviously it's at the rink, so you've got to spend another weekend at the rink. If I'm on tour, Rocky has to come on tour to see me, and he's gotta hang around the rink again. It feels a bit like work. You don't feel "off."

We never said, "Oh, let's skate together." We always said, "Let's *never* skate together." I dated Lloyd, and Rocky [dated his] first partner, so we both know what it is to date your partner, and that's not always easy. We just decided to not ever, ever mix skating with personal life. We just like doing our skating and coming back home [New Jersey] to each other.

I don't know if being married to a skater is better than [being married] to a nonskater, but it's definitely better than being with someone from another sport. The experience I had [with a former boyfriend who was a freestyle skier] was that we were never at the same place at the same time. His sport was never quite the same season. He would come home and I would leave for tour, and vice versa—I would come home from tour and it was time for him to go for training camp.

Another person at home—who wasn't an athlete—it might be hard for them, but it might be easier for me because every time I went home I would know I would have someone there. The advantage of another skater is that sometimes we are at the same place together. Athletes understand that you are totally in love with your sport. They understand why the sport takes such a place in your life. If you date someone who has a job, or someone who is more at home, they don't understand why you want to be on the road, why you want to do this sport so far away.

Having someone from the same sport definitely helps, because Rocky totally understands what I'm going through and I understand what he's going through.

But even then, it's hard.

MANDY WÖTZEL

Breaking Up Is Hard to Do

After a star-crossed career marked by spectacular injuries and attacks of nerves at exactly the wrong time, Mandy Wötzel and Ingo Steuer finally won the World Pairs Championship in 1997. They had been second twice, and their victory capped an outstanding season in which they also won the Grand Prix (Champions Series) Final and three fall internationals.

It could be that part of the reason they had such a successful year was that they had brought an end to their off-ice liaison and had come to grips with their altered relationship. They had become "an item" after the 1993 Worlds, but decided to break it off during the 1995–96 season. There was an adjustment period, during which disputes about skating would get personal and angry enough that their coach, Monica Scheibe, would leave the ice, but by the 1996–97 season, they were handling their new circumstances well.

Wötzel says that it's perfectly understandable why skating partners would also be drawn toward an off-ice relationship. Confidence in and dependency upon the other person are necessities on the ice, especially in the dangerous pairs discipline, and they're pretty good assets upon which to build a social connection, as well.

Without trust you cannot skate together. On the throws and lifts, you have to be together. One partner alone is nothing. I think some partners could maybe be boyfriend and girlfriend, too. It depends what kind of people you are. Really quiet people, it could be. But we are both strong characters, so we fight more when we are together. When we came off the ice we fought the whole time, about skating. And that's not good, because you cannot relax from skating, and that's what you need if you want to be good at it. So I suppose it's better if you don't stay together outside of skating.

I think it comes back to what I was saying about trust. If you trust a person on the ice, maybe you trust him in life. Maybe that's not right. It was a hard time breaking up, but it was a good time for me. I learned a lot about people, I learned a lot about me. It was a hard time, but now we are through it and now we feel better. We learned a lot and we feel very good like this.

The pairs team could break up over that kind of thing. If you're not strong enough, it could. It was a hard time to go through, because sometimes you get such a fight.

The Russian teams are often couples off the ice, too…maybe they have another mentality. It's not just the pairs teams—it's the dance teams. And even the singles get together.

ELENA BECHKE

Friendship and Business

Elena Bechke and Denis Petrov began their pairs partnership in 1987, in what is now St. Petersburg, Russia, then known as Leningrad. Confronted by a powerful Soviet pairs hierarchy that included, among others, Gordeeva and Grinkov, Valova and Vasiliev, Mishkuteniok and Dmitriev and Shishkova and Naumov, they managed to progress quickly up the ranks, until they were 1989 World bronze medalists, 1992 national champions and 1993 Olympic silver medalists before turning professional. They are known for several original moves, including their signature death spiral, "The Impossible," designed by their legendary coach, Tamara Moskvina, with whom they still train.

They plan to reduce their touring schedule after the 1997–98 season "so that we can live a normal life. Both of us," says Bechke. Those lives will include teaching at the new arena in Richmond, Virginia.

They were secondary pairs headliners with Stars on Ice, but after the death of Sergei Grinkov, they moved into the featured pairs role for 1996–97, a move that coincided with their best pro competitive season. They won the Canadian Professional Championships, and for the first time since 1992 were World Pro champions.

The revived competitive success was no coincidence, Bechke theorizes. After three years of dating and five years of marriage, the couple divorced in 1995 and soon their skating improved.

The difference is big, now that we are not married. I think that our relationship has improved a lot, because now we're more friends and we care about each other much more, because the love is not there anymore. It's just simple friendship. Friendship and lots of care.

Now we realize we need each other for work and for business. We have something for each other, but there is no way that it is going to change back.

With Denis and I, it was happening all the time that we took the home to the rink and the rink to the home. We didn't manage to split those things. Most of the time, if I was upset on the ice, I was upset off the ice, and then we were going home and I was upset and I couldn't sleep. And next morning I was upset again. So it was like a circle, and I couldn't find the exit. It affected our relationship very much.

When we were amateurs we were very much together because we had the same goals and the same desire to do well at the Worlds and the Olympics. And then when we accomplished that, we sort of felt well, okay let's look around a little bit. Because when we were amateurs we didn't have life. We had only skating.

And then we both looked around and we figured out that we got married a little bit too early for both of us. We were not ready. It wasn't a marriage of convenience... but I would say it was sort of. We were together all the time. We loved each other. Everything seemed perfect.

There was no pressure [from the Russian Federation] to get married, not at all. I would say I felt more pressure from my mom and dad, because I was getting so old. In Russia, if you're 24 and you're not married it's, like, "Well, okay, isn't it *time?*"

I think when we started to have trouble, it affected our skating because we were fighting a lot and I didn't manage to save my nerves for competitions. I needed him to support me. [To say things] like, "Don't worry. Don't be nervous. Everything's going to be okay. We're going to be fine. Don't get crazy. You'll do the triple toe." But he wasn't strong enough at the time to support me.

When you're together so much time, you do not appreciate each other as you're supposed to.

When we became pros, all of a sudden we had more free time and we said, "Okay, there's some other life besides skating," and we started looking around, and we were going in totally opposite directions. When we were amateurs, we didn't have time to talk about that.

Work has always helped us to go through our troubles. That energy you have inside yourself, that anger, goes into it. As soon as we became professionals, we learned to compromise a lot.

Now skating is okay, but everything else is really painful. You know, you spend eight years of your life with this person and then you see him going out with somebody else and it's sort of, you know, "Why? Wasn't I good enough?" When I go out with someone else, I feel really uncomfortable. It's weird, because I try to sneak out. I don't want Denis to see me going out with somebody. It just really feels awkward. If I feel pain, then I know he feels pain.

When we're on the road, we don't go out with people because we're too busy skating, and if we do go out, we go out with people from Stars on Ice as a group. I think we both can't wait until we are done with traveling, when we will not see each other every day.

When we split the marriage it made us better skaters because we stopped fighting about private things. Now it's more like friendship and business. Skating.

We were always second in the pro competitions. Second was always our place, no matter who else was first. We could not win because we were not concentrating on skating. We were sort of lost in our feelings and emotions.

But since then, we concentrate on skating because we put away our past. We have managed to get through it. Over.

Skating as a
Full-Time Job

MICHAEL ROSENBERG

The Battle Has Become Enjoined

It has become clear that before the peace, there will be more war. Its grip on the sport, if not its very existence, threatened by the explosion in professional skating triggered by the Lillehammer Olympics, the International Skating Union—and its individual members—has accelerated efforts to keep top stars in the amateur world as long as possible.

Better marketing, more competitions, bigger purses and a far more aggressive attitude are the stamps of the new approach from the leadership of the amateur world.

The most extreme example might have occurred at the World Team Championship in September 1966, when the USFSA sought a $1,000 sanction fee for the participating flower girls who were connected to USFSA programs.

Michael Rosenberg, who has been a skater's agent, mostly at the professional level for two decades, is a keen observer of what International Figure Skating *magazine calls "The New Cold War."*

The amateur world of the ISU has become extremely, deadly, competitive with the professional world. The premise is that whoever controls the skaters controls the sport. If the ISU can make it so attractive for skaters to stay "eligible" because they can make a lot of money, why move to professional? They can be in good events. They can get tremendous publicity. They can have careers.

[The ISU] controls the skaters. Their events become big events instead of small events. [The ISU] has their television contracts, and those contracts require that X number of name skaters, title skaters, be in the event, or the television network would feel it was a breach of contract. The ISU cannot say it's going to have Skate America, Skate Canada, Skate Whatever and have nobody there, so it has to control the skaters as much as it can. Which means that the whole professional world—which is the Dick Button competitions, the IMG competitions, the Jefferson Pilot competitions, Ice Capades, Disney on Ice, Torvill and Dean touring show, Nutcracker touring show, Gershwin on Ice touring show, all the amusement parks with their shows, all the club shows, etc., etc., etc.—are in very very deadly competition with the amateurs as to who controls what.

It's the same in any sport, whether it's tennis, golf, baseball, football or whatever. Look at basketball. There used to be the rule that you couldn't play pro until your class graduated. The NCAA [National Collegiate Athletic Association] said it was trying to keep kids in school. But the reality was that it was trying to control the athletes. You can't draw big crowds, big TV ratings, if your biggest star from Michigan is now playing for the Pistons.

So the control of the skaters is everything. And that's a dramatic change in our sport.

It's very, very argumentative now. Who are the biggest stars in the skating world, if you and I walked into a grocery store and asked people?

In the old days, you would name Dorothy Hamill, Peggy Fleming, Scott Hamilton, Katarina Witt, Robin Cousins, etc., etc.

Now you look at Scott Hamilton, Kristi Yamaguchi, Katia Gordeeva, Torvill and Dean, Katarina Witt, etc. Are those the biggest names in the sport? You could make a good argument that they are.

The other argument is uh-uh, the biggest names in the sport are Elvis Stojko, Tara Lipinski, Michelle Kwan. Especially heading into the Olympics. The amateur side gets the most publicity, and gets it on the sports side.

Who is bigger, Scott Hamilton or Elvis Stojko? You can make good arguments both ways. Maybe right now, the pendulum is more toward Scott. It used to be *way* toward Scott. Now it's not. And it would now be way toward Michelle Kwan and Lu Chen versus toward Kristi Yamaguchi.

There is much more parity. The fight has become enjoined.

JOSÉE CHOUINARD

A Different Kind of Pressure

Despite the fact that she was Canadian champion three times, Josée Chouinard is often criticized for what she was not: a medalist at the World Championships. Had Chouinard delivered again any of the free skates that won her a national title—most notably the seamless routine of 1993—a month later, she would have stood on the World podium. But she did not, and never finished higher than fifth at the global level.

And that bothered—still bothers—the elegant athlete from Rosemont,

Quebec, far more than it bothered any of her detractors. Fifth in the world is a commendable placing, but more was expected of Chouinard because of her potential. She had "the complete package": jumps, spins, speed, artistic flair, great beauty. She expected more of herself.

So when she turned professional after the 1994 Olympics, it lasted only six months. She was encouraged by strong showings at some pro competitions, including a stunning victory at the inaugural Canadian Professional Championships, and felt that she had a firmer grip on her self-esteem. She felt she deserved to be considered among the world's best and wanted to prove it. So, with the World Championships scheduled for Canada, 1995–96 seemed like a good year to reinstate herself. With a solid fall season and good practice sessions, it looked like the right decision—until a disastrous nationals, when she was decisively beaten by upstart Jennifer Robinson. Canada could send only one woman to Worlds, and it was not going to be Chouinard.

Chouinard, as was the plan, then returned to the pros, touring with Stars on Ice and rebounding emotionally with some good performances in professional competitions.

She seems much more at ease in the professional ranks than she did in the more nerve-racking amateur world.

I feel a lot more comfortable, actually. I loved the challenge in the amateur world, but the pressure was different. I think it's maybe only me who sees it differently. It's my job now. It takes off a lot of pressure, because the way I see it, I have a good day at work, then I get a promotion—in the pro competition. But if it doesn't go well, it's just a bad day at the office. Professionally, you have more opportunities. And that's a difference from amateur. In amateur, you have the international fall competitions, but let's say you do not do well at divisionals or nationals, then it stops there. You don't go any further. In professional, they're pretty much all separate. You get invited to a competition and you know that whatever happens there you're still going to the next one, because you were also invited. It doesn't stop because of one competition. You only [compete if you] get invited, so you know in advance which ones you're going to. It's a different kind of pressure. When I was an amateur I couldn't compare the two, so I didn't know that I didn't like it.

A lot of people could say that I had a great career. A lot of ladies would like to have three national titles, but I'm still looking at it where I wanted more.

When I came back amateur, for once I didn't see nationals as where I had to be at my peak. For once I really believed in myself, and I was looking at Worlds. I think that's a little bit what happened, because normally when I was at nationals I was at my peak and I was doing amazing practices. I was skating flawless, and I'd get to the competition and I'd have a lot more confidence. The year I came back, I knew my peak had to be at Worlds, because those were my goals. For the first time I really believed that I could step on that podium. Before everybody believed in me, but I didn't . . . not that much, anyway. I think that's why I was almost scared to go on the podium. I always skated well in the short program at Worlds, always. If you talk to other skaters, probably the short program is the most stressful one, but it was never my problem. But for me, I'd be so close to the podium after the short program that it almost scared me.

Then that year I came back, for the first time I was ready for it and believed in myself and that I should be there. And then I got to nationals and I wasn't practicing as well because I wasn't peaking. And I didn't skate my best. This time the approach was totally different and it didn't work out there . . . and it stopped there.

I could have gained a lot. For me, it's still hard, but I'm very good about it right now. My skating is going so well and I'm happy where I am. It's only when I look back that it still hurts.

As far as my confidence, I've gained it back, but it was hard. I've had my best tour with Stars on Ice since I've been with them, and the more I've been competing in professional, the better I became. I never really skated consistently five times in a row, but with the Ladies Series [in late 1996] I did it, so I was really, really happy.

I'm happy to be a professional. It would have happened even if I had been on the podium at Worlds. That was my decision. I wanted to go professional after that one year back. This is where I felt the most comfortable. But I had something to accomplish first.

It didn't happen, and I still have a little bit of [regret] about it. But I'm working hard on it and I've come a long way since that year. It's hard to learn from such a bad experience, but you normally learn more from a bad one than a good one.

Figure skating is such a tricky sport. You have four minutes, and if it doesn't happen then, it's over. You don't accumulate points, or you're not judged by what you're able to do. I skated so well the year I came back in all my internationals, plus I was on the podium in the Grand Prix Final, a week after nationals, where I was totally out of it. One competition cost me a lot, whereas the whole year I skated so well.

Professional is totally different. You don't have that one competition that brings you to the World Championship. When you're on tour, if you have a bad show, the next day you have another show. But you can't have very many, because it's your reputation, and your career is based on how you skate. If you skate bad all the time, it's not going to be a long career.

So the pressure is still there, but your whole year of training is not based on one competition. And that's what's different.

JANET KNIGHT

Life on the Road

One of the major themes of the sixties was "On the Road," and that's exactly where Janet Knight spent them. On the road with Ice Capades.

Knight (born Janet Runn) grew up in New Jersey before moving to California at the age of 11. Ironically, it was in the warm-weather state that she learned the sport. She skated at several rinks in the Los Angeles area, but the one that had the most effect was run by René Desjardins. He didn't teach amateurs, just skaters who wanted to become professionals or who wanted to skate for fun. He taught all the show tricks: split jumps, the flip-and-a-half lunge, the Arabians, the Charlotte, the butterfly, illusions, high kicks—"Anything that had anything of a show or a dance feel to it," Knight recalls.

She had been skating only two years, when she was asked to do what then constituted a professional show. It was a tough decision, but she didn't want to devote all her time to the sport, and that's what amateur skating demanded in those days of compulsory figures. Besides, the rink was a long drive from her house, and being 13 already, she probably didn't have a big future in amateur competition.

Eventually, she joined Ice Capades and met her future husband, Don Knight, who was Canadian champion and who had finished third at the 1965 Worlds. Although they skated a few production numbers opposite each other as male and female leads, they were never a formal pairs team. They were married in 1969 and skated with Capades until 1971, then left the road for two years to teach skating in Santa Monica, California. Then they toured in Europe for three years, until Ice Capades asked them to rejoin the show for the 1976–77 season. Just prior to that, Janet became pregnant with their first child, Kelly, and took the year off from skating. "So I sold programs, instead." They stayed with Ice Capades until 1980, when they moved to Canada.

I t's the mid-1950s and I'm 13 and at a point where it's time for a decision— do I want to go into amateur skating, which was late at that point to start to get heavy into school figures, or do I want to turn professional because there was a chance to do this show at the Beverly Hills Hotel? I talked it over with my mom and we went the professional route.

René put together a tank show for the graduation party of Glendale High School. He had a few of his students participate. So that did it. Once you accepted money in those days, that did it. Twenty-five dollars. It probably felt like a lot of money in those days.

I went through high school and didn't do anything else professionally. Just skated, with maybe the idea of joining a show someday. I went to college one year, and during that year Rosemary and Bob Dench came to the Culver City Arena during one of my practice sessions. They were the L.A. scouts for Ice Capades. I guess René had mentioned there was somebody he wanted them to look at. I didn't know this, because I was saying I wasn't ready to go in the show, I didn't want to do this. Actually, I was scared to death to audition. I was running through my program one day and I saw them at the side of the rink. I'm skating my number and I'm saying to René, "They're aud-*ition*-ing me!" Through that, they accepted me as an understudy the next season. I joined Ice Capades in 1964, skating in a line and doing understudy work.

The pro life got better as it went along. When I first joined the show in 1964, it was very stuffy, very snobby. The principals didn't talk to the line kids. Not only were they not talking to the line, they wouldn't even talk to each other, that's how competitive it was. It was a very tense atmosphere...a star regime. But that sort of changed over the years.

It started to break down when Ann-Margaret Frei, the Swedish champion came, and she was nice to everybody, talked to everybody. And that drove the other ones *cra*-zy. You know, how could you break the code? That started it, and as the years went by the new kids coming in wouldn't take that kind of stuff. Those kids just changed, and it was much better for that.

I was one of the lucky ones, I didn't have a weight problem. Weigh-in was once a week...always Saturday morning. It was terrible. A lot of kids come on the road after being at home, where they had regular times for eating and Mom would fix the dinner and it would be good food. But they'd come to the show, and finish so late at night. They're starving, [so they] go out to eat, go to sleep, and they don't wear it off. They'd eat a lot of junk food, and they'd party a lot. It all adds up.

It was a real worry for some of the kids. They'd end up hurting themselves by taking too many laxatives and trying to get on diet pills. Thursday was their cutoff. They couldn't eat after the show and they'd start taking laxatives because they knew that Saturday morning was coming. At first there used to be a fine system—if you were overweight, or you were late, or you didn't wear a piece of the costume you were supposed to. Then they fought that with unions, so it got to be warnings—you'd get three warnings and you were out. I don't know what's happening now.

When I first joined the show it was $125 a week. And I think I got another $15 or $20 when I understudied. You paid for your own hotels, you paid for your own food, but they did help you out with hotel rates. I think it was, like, $4.25 or $4.50 a night, double occupancy. You'd always try to get a roommate to cut down on the costs.

It was not easy trying to budget all that. You took the job more for the traveling and experience. Once you got up the ladder, the money got better . . . but nothing like it is today. The skating was the best part . . . to get a job you enjoy so much and get paid for it, at 18, was a thrill.

No more studying and no more books. Doing what made you feel good.

BARBARA ANN SCOTT-KING

Thank You, Avery

Avery Brundage, the longtime International Olympic Committee president from Chicago, was never liked in Canada. People in the Canadian hockey world didn't agree with many of his decisions and he made an entire city completely crazy when he thunderously enforced the strict amateur code of the day in the case of Barbara Ann Scott. Amateurs were expected to be exactly that. Only pros made money. Amateurs either already had money or found ways, not even remotely connected to sport, to raise funds for training and living expenses.

It seems that the only Canadian who appreciated his action was Barbara Ann herself.

In 1947, when I got back after winning the World Championship, the people of Ottawa gave me a yellow car. I said, "I can't accept this, but it's beautiful." And they said, "Oh, yes, you can. It's all cleared." Which it wasn't. Avery Brundage spoke right up about it, and I had to give it back right away.

The next year at Olympics in St. Moritz, I saw him and he said, "I suppose you hate me!" I said, "No, Mr. Brundage, I'm eternally grateful to you. If you had waited until now, what would I have done? I wouldn't have been allowed to compete in the Olympics."

My father always taught me that if you're going to play a game, play by the rules or don't play. And those rules were very well stated in those days—nothing over $25 for an amateur . . . or that's it!

BRIAN ORSER

Changing Gears

In every professional sport one of the operative words is adaptation. Usually, it has to do with an athlete having to continually adjust to the altered strategies of his opponent.

In Brian Orser's case, that opponent had many faces: time, new stars, his talent representatives, his own emotions. He forthrightly confesses that he had become alternately complacent with and angry about his professional career.

But a true professional adapts. Not only must the show go on, but so must you. To Orser's credit, he not only recognized what was going wrong, he admits it out loud. And he worked hard at correcting it and getting his career back on track.

From the outside, the professional world looks easier to handle than the training-based amateur world. But it's got its own harsh realities, and every pro learns about them.

One thing I have learned is that the squeaky wheel gets the oil. If you allow yourself to get swept under the carpet, you will be. I just have to keep reminding myself, and reminding my agent, and reminding the public that these are my credentials—this is what I've done, and it's pretty good. And that I'm still out there.

Things have changed. When I first turned pro, I thought, "You go out and do shows. People pay money to see you skate. And that's that. Do a few double toe loops and call it a day."

But not anymore. And it changed in midstream for me. All of a sudden, boom!—everybody's out there. Now you're out there with the amateurs and all your other friends who are pro. Everyone's skating great and you have to keep up.

Scott Hamilton was a little bit in the rut that I was in, and then one year he pulled up his socks and went for it. He came back with triple flip, which he hadn't done since the 1984 Olympics. He nailed the triple Lutz every time. He was doing the odd triple toe–triple toe combination, which he had never done before. So he came back 10 years or more later as good or better than he was in 1984.

You have to figure out which direction you're going to go. If you're going to just go out there and be a "skating whore," doing everything—which is what I did—then don't expect to skate well. You've got to build practice into your skating schedule and just not take on everything. You'll have a weekend when you can stay at home and train, or do a show and make 10 grand. I would [say], "Oh, 10 grand. That'll be nice. That'll pay some more taxes, or this or that. I'll take the 10 grand." You know what I mean?

Now I've learned. Your best voice to express that you are still out there is to skate well. And that's what I've been doing. I've been working my way back up and back in, and being credible. I had put on weight and I knew I wasn't performing. But you don't know which comes first, the chicken or the egg. I was feeling down because I didn't feel I was getting support from my agency, which resulted in the way I was skating. And the lack of support resulted from my skating. I didn't think I was getting the proper representation as a two-time Olympic silver medalist and World champion. I didn't think my name was out there, and I wasn't getting a great spot in the show. But that was because I wasn't skating well. But I wasn't skating well because I was feeling like crap.

My self-esteem hit an all-time low around 1992, when some of the new skaters came along and I was quickly under the carpet. And I hated that. I didn't want to skate well anymore.

I got some help from Scott Hamilton and Tracy Wilson. A kick in the ass. They were very frank and right to the point. It wasn't time to be stroking me. It was time to say, "This is what you've done. This is how good you are. This is what you're capable of. You've got to lose some weight. You can't party as much, and you've got to be focused, the way you were in 1988." That's the only way you can do it now. This is the entertainment business and you can be out there, going out night after night after the show for a few drinks and food.

So I had to go on a diet. I had put on 30 pounds, and fat don't fly. Gravity pulls that stuff down fast. I'll never be Olympic weight again—that's kid stuff. But now I feel comfortable again. On tour I feel I belong there. I really get a good hand. Hopefully the aftermath will be that people will be talking about me when they leave the show. They'll be talking about Kurt—maybe they paid to see Kurt—but they'll be talking about me, too, when they leave.

In 1988, I sort of thought I'd be pro for five years. And here I am 10 years later, still liking it.

And just sort of changing gears.

ELIZABETH MANLEY

The Hardest Job of My Life

When you come up big in the Olympics, the world is your oyster. Liz Manley had several career options awaiting her after she won the free skate and finished second overall at the Calgary Olympics. Although joining Ice Capades exhausted her, she does not regret her choice.

I went into the long haul of Ice Capades, which a lot of people frowned upon. Here I am, Canada's sweetheart, Olympic silver medalist, and I'm running to an American show with Smurfs and California Raisins and things like that.

It was a childhood dream of mine to go to Ice Capades, because it was a show I went to as a child. It was the hardest job I've done in my life. In three seasons with Ice Capades, I did over a thousand shows.

I learned how to survive. I really learned how to live and to take care of myself, to fight the back-stabbing kind of show business world. I gained a tough skin in Ice Capades and I knew, through my experience there, I could get through anything. And I think that's why, nine years later, I am where I am.

Ice Capades really was a hard lesson to learn. It was being thrown into an experience where I no longer had the security of home and family and coaches to get me out of situations. I didn't have my entourage, so to speak. I had to fight for myself. I had to fight through 15 shows a week. I had to do it sick, healthy, injured, and it gave me a tough skin.

Everybody in the United States knew me as the little blonde with the white cowboy hat who beat Debi Thomas. Nobody could put a name to the person. And my three years in Ice Capades made me a household name in America. As hard as it was for me to be taken away from Canada a lot—I didn't get to perform there nearly as much as I wanted to or begged to—it gave me a career in the U.S. And as we have to admit, that's where the money is and where a lot of the skating work is.

Nine years later, I'm being asked to do American pro competitions [as much as I am] Canadian competitions. So, as brutal as Ice Capades was, and as hard work as it was, it laid the groundwork for me as a professional.

KERRY LEITCH

Pro in One, Pro in 'Em All

Kerry Leitch is president of the International Professional Skating Union, the umbrella organization for full-time coaches, which was formed during the 1963 World Championships. The IPSU also provides the judges for many of the major professional competitions. It's Leitch's hope to start a school for professional judges so that there is some kind of common ground to the wide variety of formats promoters keep inventing for pro competition.

A man with a keen sense of humor, Leitch is nevertheless a strong disciplinarian in his role as head coach at the Preston Figure Skating Club and director of the Champions Training Centre. And it works. Throughout the 1980s, his school was the place in Canada to come for pairs training, and it still provides a good share of the country's top tandems. He's had dozens of national champions and several World medalists. Lloyd Eisler, among many others, began his pairs career there, and current contenders Jodeyne Higgins and Sean Rice train under Leitch.

The club's annual spring carnival is one of the best and most elaborate in North America.

While he's a determined and demanding skating mentor, completely dedicated to his sport, Leitch is also in a decided minority: figure skating people who are fully cognizant of what's going on in other sports. He'd feel just as at home in baseball spikes as in figure skates. In fact, his professional future once appeared to be in baseball, not figure skating. It was only because he was so good at baseball that he became a skating pro—in the days when "skating pro" meant coaching for money.

I signed with the New York Yankees in 1958, when I was 17. I was still skating and playing baseball in the summers, which I always did. In the middle of August they sent me to Toronto to join up with the Richmond Virginians, who were then the Yankees' triple-A farm team. I was a catcher. It was the last weekend of the season, so I finished the season with them and then I was going to go back and skate.

I was thinking of competing one more year. I had competed in junior nationals, but had never competed in senior Canadians as a single skater. I was second last [in juniors]. I can't remember who I beat, but one of the guys who beat me was skating for therapy because he had broken his back. I felt that I got ripped off because I should have beaten this one guy with the bad back. [The decision] was a 4–3 split. It was just poor judging.

I was going to compete in seniors, but then I found out that if you were professional in one sport, you were professional in them all. I think I got something like a $1,500 bonus, something small. I got traded into the St. Louis Cardinals chain, and partway through the season I went down to Rochester at the same time they signed [future Hall of Famer] Tim McCarver. They signed him for 150 grand. I was a catcher—he was a catcher—so the writing was on the wall. Then I decided that I was just going to teach skating, because I couldn't go back to skate in amateur.

So the decision was kind of made for me. My first love was baseball, and I probably would have loved to do that. It's still one of my loves. In retrospect, I don't have any problem with what I ended up doing. I've enjoyed being in the teaching business, but I maybe didn't plan on doing it that young.

It's true that not many figure skating people are involved, or interested, in other sports. I think that there are a limited few who enjoy golf, but as far as actively participating in other sports...not many. I think it's part of the old-wives' tale that as a figure skater you always had to be careful not to get injured. But I played junior hockey. I played basketball. I played football. I just think I wasn't one of the kids who was worried about hurting himself.

The other thing was that you tried to participate in the other sports to prove that you weren't a little "strange" because you figure-skated. That handle was hung on skaters, certainly when I skated. Maybe not as prevalent as now, but it certainly was there. I got grief all the time. But I played other sports, and I've always been big, and I didn't have any of the artistic qualities—I never took ballet—so I never ever skated fancy. I skated the same way I did everything else—I was pretty aggressive—I was able to prove myself as an athlete, which helped. And playing hockey helped an awful lot, too, plus the fact that the line we had in peewee hockey scored more than anyone else had ever scored in minor hockey up to that point.

I took figure skating only because I wanted to play hockey. I was 10 years old, living in Woodstock, Ontario, and my mother, who is a very aggressive person, said, "If you're going to play hockey you're going to learn to skate, so you're going to go into a figure skating club." I said, "No bloody way." And so the next day I joined the figure skating club." She dragged me down there. I realized I wasn't going to win that one.

And the only reason I stayed was I thought the odds were pretty good. I was the only guy in the club with about 150 girls. Actually, I enjoyed it, because I loved the athletic part of jumping. I never worked that much on spins or footwork. I just loved to jump.

I was fortunate all the way through that there weren't many male skaters and the skaters there were, were very athletic. Greg Folk was one. Greg liked to toss the baseball around. You don't see that now. Kurt [Browning] was sort of like that. He brought that back. He likes to play hockey. He can throw a spiral probably 60 yards. He loves to play golf, I think he got a hole-in-one the first time playing golf. Mike Slipchuk is another one [who is] pretty athletic. It goes through waves, or whatever.

That's why I always stayed in the sport—because I never had the problem of anybody hanging too much of a handle on me for being effeminate and I didn't attract the sort of artistic group in skating.

ROBIN COUSINS

Why Not Ice Theater Competition?

Robin Cousins skated his final competitive program in December of 1995, on home ice in England.

His generation was one of the most remarkable in men's skating. From 1973 to 1979, the World Championship was won by six different men, and a seventh, Cousins, won the 1980 Olympics.

Cousins has turned his considerable creative talents to the theatrical world.

Our era? It ain't going to happen again. There's too much too soon now. We had to work so hard to get to a championship. We then had to prove ourselves at the championship to get into the exhibition on Sundays. We then had to prove ourselves in the exhibition for the privilege of being asked on the tour. There was no money involved. We did it because we loved it.

This is my 25th year of international performing. Toller is still out there. Dorothy still skates. Scott is still skating. Tai and Randy are still skating. People still want to see us skate. And I don't belittle anything that these skaters have now, and they are phenomenal. But I'm just wondering, 10 to 15 years from now, (a) will they be around? and (b) how many people will still want to see them skate?

I have to be perfectly honest. Because [competing] is still not so far away from me, there is some sort of jealousy that we missed out on some of the stuff coming around for pros now. And I don't necessarily mean monetarily, but in terms of exposure. We had to fight for our sport to get exposure, and a lot of great things got missed. And now everything and its mother is on television.

They are trying desperately to get the professionals and the amateurs together, but unlike tennis, which is the same game whether you're on grass or clay, professional and amateur figure skating are not the same game. What you can do as a professional has *no* bearing on what these kids are doing as amateurs.

With the popularity of skating and the scope of visibility, both network and theatrically, wouldn't you think people would want to expand the sport rather than try to conform it and contract it?

There are skaters who can skate on a 40-foot patch of ice and mesmerize, whom you wouldn't think about watching in an arena. And vice versa. There are people who can skate only on big ice—you wouldn't want to put them on a tank.

But there's no reason you couldn't put nine judges in the second row of the Royal Alex in Toronto, with ice on the stage, and have a theatrical skating competition.

I would have thought skating people would say, "Oh, you're right. What a great idea!" But they look at you as if you're nuts.

JOANNE VINCENT

A Career…with Ears

Playing Mickey Mouse in Walt Disney's World on Ice makes for an unusual juxtaposition of fame and anonymity. Everyone knows your character; no one knows you.

Joanne Vincent coaches in Burlington, Ontario. She also choreographs and directs the successful ice carnivals there—a skill she attributes directly to her four-year career with Disney on Ice.

As an amateur, Vincent competed at the novice level but never qualified for nationals. Nevertheless, she's got flair and style. Extroverted and funny, she was a perfect choice to play the star the Disney empire was built upon.

She says that teaching is the joy of her life: "Not teaching the skating, so much as teaching the life skills." And so she is straightforward when asked about life in a major touring show. Yes, it's great to be Mickey, and yes, it's great to travel. But there are subtle pitfalls you must guard against, including skating's notorious fixation with weight control—a fixation that can encourage eating disorders.

My sister, Patty, had been skating with Disney for four years. It created a little curiosity, more than anything, in me, since I was going to go into phys. ed. at university. After I auditioned several times in Buffalo, Disney continued to call me to join. But my mind was pretty set on going to university.

Then, at the very last minute, I chose to go the show. It was an opportunity. It came down to the wire and I said, "Nope, I really want to see what my sister does." We're very close.

Patty and I had completely different goals when it came to the ice show. When I got there I knew exactly what my goal was—to enjoy life, the freedom to experience, being who I wanted to be and letting go. With school and skating, school and skating, [my life had been] regimented. This was my opportunity to be free and do as I pleased.

I was absolutely reckless. Patty, however, wasn't. She was determined to climb the ladder within Disney and she did. She became female line captain, and presently is performance director. It's her 14th year, whereas I lasted four years.

I was pushing things to the limit, and I wasn't the only one. [The skaters were] all competitors who pounded hard hours, at the time [1986], making $400 U.S. right out of high school. The freedom was tremendous. You had this money. You were traveling North America.

It was the first year they did Snow White on Ice, but it's a requirement that Mickey Mouse be in every show. I walk into the situation and they typecast me as Mickey Mouse.

An instant celebrity.

The treatment of Mickey Mouse, who is the world's greatest celebrity—I can't begin to tell you! It was so overwhelming. From this little high school to that—you can only imagine the major transition that took place.

I was treated like gold. I was given so much, from dinners to gifts, to rides in limousines. From publicists, mayors, children . . . any human being who was touched by Mickey Mouse, which is everyone. I was Mickey on the ice and in many publicity appearances—hospitals, senior-citizens homes.

There are rules for being Mickey Mouse. First and foremost, you absolutely cannot talk, because it's Disney policy that those characters have particular voices and no one else does them. But I didn't need to talk, my movement was so believable. I was trained to develop animation, and I knew I could get the point across without words. We'd always have a skater or some representative with us who would do any conversation that was necessary. But I knew I could get the point across.

Just looking at these characters, you know exactly what I mean by their liveliness. Just in the facial structure, the paint and the expression, the characters are so believable in the first place. Second, I was trained by Jerry Bilik, who made me exactly what I was, as far as Mickey goes. My head was never high enough, never strong enough, never large enough. He squeezed so much out of me, right down to the last day. It was an unbelievable experience.

Before I went in, I had no concept, no idea of Mickey, but it felt very natural. And they said, "That's exactly why we typecast. We could feel that energy in your personality." I'd throw that head on and I'd know exactly what my movement was. Jerry was able to enhance that. It's just in me.

Today, often I'll be called up by local publicists if the show comes to town, whether it's Buffalo or Hamilton, and they're in need of advance publicity. I put on the suit and [becoming Mickey] is just an automatic thing, even after seven years out of [the show].

I have kids I teach today, 18 or 19 years old, who say, "I want to join a show. What's it all about?" and I have to give my most honest answer. And my most honest answer is, it's a tremendous experience. And that includes both positive and negative.

Some of my most positive experiences came from that show. The fame, tremendous moments with celebrities from Kurt Russell to Susan Lucci to Mario Lemieux. Amazing experiences.

On the other hand, some of my worst experiences came from the show. Relationships. You became confined in a company of maybe 100, 150, people. So you're in a very lonely lifestyle on the road, and instantly [the company] is your family. So you tend to reach out for comfort, and often relationships result, and often abusive relationships occur. Mine wasn't a pleasant one, by any means. It was what I considered one of my most unpleasant experiences.

Certainly the weight situation was, as well. My sister always laughs about the day I walked in and said, "Why is everyone so wound up about these weekly weigh-ins?" and she said, "You'll see."

It becomes a problem. I'd never had an eating disorder in my life. I'd never even thought about food. But it has to become something you're concerned about, because it's your job. You have to weigh in within a six-pound range—mine was 104 to 110—every week.

There were areas of it that did affect me, but not to the degree that it affected some of my friends. Rooming with three other girls, from bulimics to anorexics, who were addicted to exercise and/or laxatives and/or starving and binging or dehydrating or whatever—those were the facts of life. If they had the problem before [joining] the show, I think it was only enhanced. As I step outside of [the experience], I think most of them had family problems. All struggled, generally, with that control situation of parents running their lives for so long through skating. And all of a sudden they were going to turn things around and say, "Yeah, well, I'm going to control this."

With me, [weight was] a problem in certain instances. Weigh-ins were Saturday, and my route was starving and binging. Wednesday you remember that weigh-ins are Saturday morning, so Wednesday, Thursday and Friday you don't eat. Saturday comes, you make your weigh-in and you eat harder and more than you ever could, on Saturday, Sunday, Monday, Tuesday. That's not a healthy eating pattern. So I think if I was affected in any way, that was definitely it. That was one of the minor problems, though.

[Playing] Mickey only added to the pressure. Promoters wanted to take me out on a Friday night and show me the best restaurants in town. Well, I had weigh-ins on Saturday morning. If I'm 110 1/4, I'm fined. Ten dollars. And at that time it was fine, fine, suspension, fired. I had many a friend who was fired for weight, either being underweight or overweight.

I knew it was a problem. It frustrated me more than ever that food was my biggest concern, that that's what I was concerned about on a daily basis.

Basically, I joined the show—I developed an eating disorder. Left the show and it ended. But it's still with you, in the background.

The day I left the show I vowed to myself that I would never, ever, ever, ever step on a scale. Ever again. Because it messed me up so badly. I even hear a scale and the tipping of it . . . it's incredible how it makes me feel.

Where Are We Going? Where Are We Now?

OTTAVIO CINQUANTA

In Search of a Better Product

When the International Skating Union met in Boston in June of 1994, its most astute members knew that the oldest international sports organization in the world was in trouble.

The ISU was rapidly losing its grip on the sport. Professional promoters, riding the popularity of the Lillehammer Olympics, were making huge inroads, threatening to strip amateur skating of all the stars who would normally graduate after the Olympics and many who would not. And the promoters were grabbing all the TV time.

The ISU had been fiddling as Rome burned. So it elected to the presidency a man who was born in Rome. Ottavio Cinquanta could, as the Chicago journalist Phil Hersh wrote, "finally bring the sport into the 20th century."

He's pretty well gotten it into the 21st century, too. Over the objections of some of the more conservative members, the ISU has instituted large prize purses for all its major events; set up a Grand Prix—both senior and junior—to add importance and context to its fall season; investigated instant replays for judges; tried to make the sport more appealing to the masses; broadened its base of membership; and challenged the professional world head-on.

Cinquanta was 55 when he was elected to the presidency. He ascended through the speed-skating side of the ISU, and that alarmed some figure skating people. But Cinquanta is a businessman (chemical and financial interests) and he knows that figure skating provides the money.

He was a sprinter on the Italian national speed skating team, and also competed in track and field. As well, he was a club ice hockey player in his youth. He and his wife, Maria Luisa, and their daughter, Consuelo, live in Milan, but he's often on the road as a member of the International Olympic Committee, the Olympic Movement Commission, the Olympic Solidarity Commission and the Coordinating Committee for the Salt Lake City Winter Games.

Cinquanta is an engaging personality, who is sometimes perceived as arrogant. But there is no doubt that he has delivered as ISU president. Yet he admits that marshaling all the divergent forces within the ISU has not been an easy task.

It's important to him that we look at the meaning of what he's saying and *not at the words—"because my English is not so good." We think it's superb, but we'll let you judge.*

It is not easy to tell you how difficult it was, how difficult it is and difficult it will be. Because this is not just related to skating or to the ISU. This is related to sport.

It is difficult because you must consider one point—federations of sport are administered like a company. But a company is in a position to produce new products, and to produce a certain range of products, you understand?

With a sport, you cannot promise to the market—you cannot produce—something, because you are unable to guarantee that what you produce next year, the next cyclist, the next runner, the next skater, is not all the time like an Eric Heiden or a Boitano. Mercedes knows it can produce next year a better car. I cannot know that next year I will have a better Michelle Kwan or a better Elvis Stojko.

So, how can we administer our international federation, using the language everybody says—but don't think about so much—that today's sport is business, today's sport is money, today's sport is like a company? They say this, but without thinking about it.

On top of that there is one point. A good president of an international federation, for a national federation, for a club, is the one who structures the federation in such a way that other people can come back and lead the club, the national federation, the international federation, under different conditions. This is not a genius—a genius is in the university in a laboratory. A good president is able to perform in such a way that administration exists, procedure exists, policy exists.

When I say I am a bit concerned, it is because I do not know if, in the near future, we will have good skaters, if there will be situations that will develop that are not under our control. The skaters on the ice are not produced by the ISU. They are produced by the clubs. You understand how far are the clubs away from me. A long way. I'm very close to the IOC, very close to the presidents of the national federations, but the clubs are something that unfortunately are very far from me.

That is why I'm interested in going very often in the dressing room. That is why I like to stand next to the athletes. They are the actors of our play. I love to stay with them. I love to talk to them. I love to create with them what I want to create—a chain with many rings. Not the Olympic rings—that is a different story. A chain made with many rings about the future. To be in a position to create the new managers, new people, guaranteeing the federation to go on, the club to go on, the family to go on.

This is life. This is my job as a president. To put in place a procedure, a structure, for them.

Next to me, side to side, there are the national federations. The clubs are under the leadership and control of the national federation. That is why I try to stay with the skaters. I try to understand and learn, every time there is a competition in speed skating, in short track, in figure skating. I try to see what I miss. It's why I try to speak to some coaches, because they tell me what is going on. They tell me what is occurring in all the venues in the world. They tell me how is the situation in Ukraine, how is the situation in Russia, in Finland, in Sweden. They tell me why Italy, one of the most important countries in the world of sport, is not in a stronger situation in figure skating.

This is what concerns me. Not because I want to criticize the international federations—I don't care about that. But because this is part of the situation of the product that Mercedes or General Motors may offer but the ISU cannot offer, the national federations cannot offer. Because you do not know—you cannot know.

USCHI KESZLER

Standing Still Is Going Backward

A basic political principle is that when confidence in the administration improves, so does the economy. Uschi Keszler, who choreographs Elvis Stojko and works with several young skaters, is opening two new rinks for hockey and skating in Aston, Pennsylvania. She had been hesitating about making the investment because of what she felt was stagnation in the figure skating world. She's changed her mind, though, since Ottavio Cinquanta took over the ISU.

As I watch the last three years since he's been the president, there have been some decisions made that were unusual for skating. Before, everything was always done on tradition, which is kind of deadly for progress. He has opened the field up so that innovation is now possible, and it's wanted. [TV executives] are looking at all kinds of different ideas and [people and] welcoming them, because they need different characters in order to cover the air time that they have. They can't have two hours and show the same thing over and over again, because TV is not going to buy that. And Cinquanta realizes that.

I feel so confident about it now that that's why we are building the two rinks in Aston. To me that's at least a 15-year commitment. I've always been one to put my money where my mouth is, but really a lot of it has to do with seeing where the ISU is going and having confidence in that.

The way it was being done before—well, the young people today, to get them interested it takes something different. You watch with the Extreme Games. You watch what they do with Rollerblades. You watch what they do with computer games. Their minds are not where our minds used to be. And to challenge them, and to have them challenged, they have to be allowed to be innovative and creative, because they are so extremely creative.

Think about it. The coaches and judges can't even start to understand what a quad feels like. Because we all did doubles. We were lucky if someone did a triple. A quad is like going to the moon and beyond. I mean, that's where it is now, and with Cinquanta, he wants to talk to the athletes. Because I think it is the athletes who have to explain to the judges what this feels like and what *is* difficult, because I don't think you can see from the outside what is difficult anymore.

Going into that next level with quads, especially quad combinations, you have to understand what you're doing. Natural talent alone doesn't get you there.

The thing is, we have the world's attention that skating is something great and that there are so many different ways of approaching it and applying it. I feel very confident right now that everybody's getting together and trying to make sure we fill the time we are getting—and the stage that we have—well, and not mess it up so that we lose the stage to someone else.

Because once you lose the stage you don't get it back.

SALLY STAPLEFORD

No Change for Change's Sake

Sally Stapleford is the first woman president of the National Ice Skating Association, the governing body for figure skating in Great Britain. She also chairs the powerful Technical Committee of the ISU, which is responsible for rules, judging and, essentially, the general direction the sport takes.

A five-time British champion and a silver medalist at the 1965 Europeans, Stapleford has also been an international judge, and has sat on scores of skating committees at both the domestic and the international level.

She has been unjustly accused of ultraconservatism by some members of the North American press. In fact, ISU president Ottavio Cinquanta says he welcomes Stapleford's balanced viewpoint amid the unstable dynamics that surround the 1990s skating world.

I think that change is good. We have to move forward. But as with anything, you must think it through. A lot of changes you think, "Oh, that's marvelous," but you haven't looked at stages two, three, four, five down the line. Obviously, you have to evolve and move on, but you also have to remember [to ask,] is it a benefit to the sport? You don't change for change's sake. It has to be a change that benefits everybody.

You'd have to ask the athletes about this, but you might have certain reservations that skaters are doing too many exhibitions, too many back-to-back competitions because of the prize money, and you might wonder, "When are they training?" Are they spending enough time having a rest period, training, peaking, and are they ever going to be as good as they can be? All right, they might be World champion, but have they ever reached their full potential, and how much better might they have been if they had rejected some of the things that came along?

It's not necessarily the Technical Committee's mandate, but the calendar maybe needs to be looked at. Some people could say that the open competitions should be out of season, from April to September, and there should be restrictions to exhibitions, especially in the season. At the end of the day, the member [country] that the skater represents also has to maybe put certain restrictions on their skater. You have to be a responsible member. They've got to ask themselves, "Are we benefitting our own skaters by allowing them to do all these things without any control?" Some members actually might be controlling—I don't know.

Yes, it's one of the concerns. You want the skating to be improving, improving, improving. You don't want to look back in four years' time and say the standards haven't gone up. Why haven't they gone up? Well, because the skaters haven't trained hard enough.

The men's event at the Worlds in 1996 was a tremendous competition and the standards have been going up, but you wonder how long the standards are going to continue to improve at the same rate if the training's not going to be done. You can't really say.

We don't see in Europe what we see on television in North America with all the pro events. It would worry me if we [ISU] went down the road of these kinds of competitions where the judging's totally unrealistic and everyone gets perfect marks, gets inflated high marks.

It worries me that the integrity of the sport would go down the hill. I think it would be very sad. After all, we are a competitive sport, and the integrity has to be retained.

DAVID DORE

A Private Industry

David Dore has been at the tiller of Canadian figure skating, almost uninterrupted, since 1980. He served a four-year term as president of the CFSA, then became its first director general.

He is one of the prime movers behind the Champions Series—or Grand Prix—an idea that originated in Canada in the mid-1980s but took until the mid-1990s to effect.

When Dore became president of the CFSA, the sport in Canada was, at best, in a holding pattern. At worst, it was in serious decline. After Karen Magnussen's World Championship in 1973, Canada landed only one World medal—a bronze by Toller Cranston—for the rest of the decade. From 1982 on, Canada has claimed at least one medal at every World Championship, and has multiple-medaled several times.

As well as developing skating talent, providing recreational outlets and administering a variety of coaching, judging and technical programs, the CFSA has turned in a new direction: event management. The Events Trust has become a huge moneymaker. Things have sure changed since 1980.

We have nine times the financial resources from that period—we are into many millions. And that came during major periods of sports stress and recession.

I think the biggest thing is the Athletes Trust, which was started really on the back of an envelope, with our fingers crossed. I'm not sure a lot of people thought it was a really good idea. It now has resources of $7 million, and it's totally self-sufficient. To me, in 17 years, that's a huge thing. We are probably the only sport in Canada that has a self-generating fund of $7 million, which is probably [giving] about a million dollars a year back to skating. It goes directly out to about 800 children, which is a lot, considering we started with only nine, at $200 each. The least a skater now would get is a couple of thousand, and it can go up to $20,000 to $25,000. It started in 1981 at Millcroft when we had that planning session. Chris Lang, Bob Howard—there were about 10 of us. It was the old guard and the new guard, and the old guard was passing.

Another big change I've seen is that there has been a real passage of the type of people. There are a lot more visionaries and a lot more action-oriented people who want to get things done. At that time [1981], I think to some extent, people were involved in the sport for the moment, instead of for the future. I think those people were there for their volunteer period. An office was meant only for day-to-day work. It wasn't for planning or visions or anything.

The national team, which came in back then, is still an entity. It's stood the test of time and become the centerpiece of television sponsorship. The entity has changed, but the sport has changed. The great thing about the national team is that it's definable by the moment, according to what it is at a certain time. It's been able to adapt to the times.

To me, in Canada television-wise, the 1988 Olympics was the real breakout point. It showed—with Brian and Brian, certainly the three ladies and the emergence of Liz and Wilson–McCall—an athletic side, an accomplished side, of our athletes, and I think that was the beginning of the star quality. Everyone in Canada still has that whole picture of Liz. From then, photographers, television, everyone, realized that you could capture a moment. It was like the

Canada–Russia hockey game. It's a moment. And then I think television found that [skating] could be made into entertainment.

At that point, I think the association also began to have confidence in its ability to be visionaries, to broaden its horizon. To become a little more aggressive. Instead of being satisfied with always being tradition, status quo, a lot more focus was on future directions. We learned how to use the stars better. We use many instead of one.

Slowly but surely, we learned to adapt and communicate to all our constituents, which included our agents and our athletes and our coaches. We've learned to bring everyone into the mix much better, and so I think we've emerged as a much more homogenized organization that really does a fair amount of listening. We used to do a lot of reacting. I don't think we stand back now and wait to see which way the wind blows. If the wind needs a slight turn, [the association] is not afraid to [provide it] anymore.

An example. We introduced a million-dollar program in the spring of 1996, the Skating Skills Program. It was six years in development because of the abandonment of figures from an external source. (And that would be another thing I'd say. Sport in Canada has been driven very much by external factors—something a lot of people just don't accept, but that's the way it is.) We fought the abandonment of figures by the ISU, for selfish reasons and because that's what our coaches said they wanted. We fought it, but when [the fight] was over, we moved on.

We were also told by our coaches to move on slowly in replacing figures, so we did. And then we created this new program. It's now been brought out that we tried to bring in the new program too...violently, I'm going to say. We tried to just stand up there and dump the program on everybody, whereas we need to stage the program in. What we're hearing is that there's nothing wrong with the program, but with our expectations. We now realize it isn't working, and we've been working frantically to adapt and readapt everything. We're not prepared to abandon it as "Well, that was a waste of a million dollars," but we are prepared to understand that it's got to be introduced a little more gradually.

We also have realized our potential as event managers. I don't think we ever realized that in the past. I always say that the night of Kurt–Elvis in Hamilton [nationals, 1993] was the huge turning of the curve. In 1990, we sold tickets to the World Championships in Halifax out of a lady's basement. In 1993, I was prepared to close off the upper bowl in Hamilton because [the event] wasn't selling in November. Then we felt if we invested $100,000 in a publicity campaign, we might sell some tickets. And we sold the rest of the place out in three weeks.

And when people came, and we saw how nuts they were and how crazy they were about everything we had to offer—the fact that we really did have product—we realized all the things around the event we could do to make it better. And slowly that developed into the Events Trust, which is the answer to no more government funding. We perceive ourselves as a private industry now. We don't perceive ourselves as a government agency at all.

MICHAEL ROSENBERG

Schlock Comes Calling

Michael Rosenberg is one of the most respected, and powerful, agents in figure skating. He and his wife, Nancy, run Marco Entertainment Inc., a management company in Palm Desert, California, which has 42 figure skating clients under contract, including Liz Manley, Rudy Galindo, Tai Babilonia and Randy Gardner.

One of Rosenberg's first clients was Ice Capades, which asked him to promote its tour in cities where it hadn't drawn well. His first individual skating client was Dorothy Hamill.

He got into figure skating in 1977 from the music industry, where he'd handled the likes of Stevie Wonder, Smokey Robinson and Aretha Franklin. He prefers skating because it's a cleaner, less ego-driven industry, but he also notices that as it grows, so does its less desirable side.

When there is so much money involved on both sides, the pro side and the amateur side—which is still the only clear-cut demarcation, not "eligible" and "ineligible" which is just nomenclature—then you see the schlock people coming out from between the cracks, trying to get into the sport.

You have no idea the calls I get—"My name is Jack So-and-So. I'm going to put together a show for Fox-TV—*Radio on Ice*." Jack wouldn't know a triple Axel from a triple Kaz-utz. All he knows is that skating gets good ratings, and radio is big in his area and nobody is doing it, so that's his shtick.

So promoters who have no love for, or interest in, anything but making money come out of the woodwork. They care nothing about the sport itself.

And agents. You get people trying to be agents or managers. You have non-skating-oriented, non-sports-oriented agents getting into the game and giving skaters and/or their parents and coaches money under the table. Money under the table, money upfront, buy them a new car, do whatever.

It's happened since 1976—Jerry Weintraub, a very famous Hollywood manager, signing Dorothy Hamill—but it's happened only at the highest level. In 1984, IMG made its first serious entree into the business by courting Scott Hamilton. He brought [the organization] full-force into skating and, of course, led it to other skaters. It became a profit center, along with the hockey, football, tennis and golf divisions that made IMG.

From 1984 until the early-1990s, [there were] basically three agent companies in skating—myself, IMG and Lee Mimms. Those were three competitors who were not adversaries and all treated one another with respect and did not try to raid one another's clients. By raiding, I'm implying when an agent goes and talks to someone else's clients—"It's greener on the other side of the fence." "I'll give you more than your present agent is giving you." In the legal profession, it's totally unethical and immoral and can get you disbarred. And potentially it is against the law, because it's third-party interference in a contract. But it's hard to prove—who went to whom? So far in our profession, there hasn't been a lawsuit—just threats and screaming. [But] it's happening more often.

DOUG BEEFORTH

The Branding of a Network

As vice president of CTV Sports, Doug Beeforth is a major power broker in figure skating. In 1997, CTV celebrated its 35th anniversary, and figure skating has been an integral part of its programming from the beginning. The network has broadcast the Canadian nationals every year and, except for a 10-year period beginning in the mid-1980s, has held the Canadian rights to the Worlds, as well. Beeforth admits that when CBC broadcast the Worlds there was an "identity crisis" at CTV.

Beeforth first got involved with skating in 1986, then jumped in with both feet when he was hired as CTV's executive producer for the host-broadcast feed at the Calgary Olympics. He was impressed by the fearless determination of skaters, and the willingness of ISU officials, particularly Joyce Hisey, to accommodate television needs. Later, he and some partners owned a company that produced CTV's sports properties. The network bought out the company in 1991 and he became vice president, CTV Sports.

I was a guy who cut my teeth, both personally and professionally, on hockey. Typical Canadian. My first and only job in television before I came [to CTV] was at *Hockey Night in Canada*. I was a dyed-in-the-wool hockey guy. And all of a sudden here I am in Calgary, and here's this other sport that until this point has been "fancy skating." In pretty quick order this sport caught me.

Figure skating has been a major part of this network's identity since virtually its beginning. There are legendary stories of Johnny Esaw having the vision in the early 1960s, of seeing this sport that at the time was not very well exposed, was not popular. Don Jackson would win a medal, but it was something you'd read in the paper. [Esaw] had the vision and foresight to say, "This is going to go somewhere." He supported the sport by putting it on television.

It has probably been the face and branding of this network as much as anything else. Figure skating is our longest-running property. We see skating as helping create what we are, and in today's world of multiple channels—anywhere from 25 to 500 channels—networks, stations, systems of stations have to have things that make their trees stand out from the forest.

Skating is attractive because it's a sport but it's also entertainment. It attracts all demographics. It's always been very strong in the female demographics, but in the last five or six years the number of men watching skating has increased. Why is that? Is it because of Browning? Possibly. Because of Elvis? Possibly.

The athletes in figure skating have never failed to impress me with their general common sense, their understanding of public relations, their general outward feeling of welcoming. I've never seen a surly figure skater, and how many stories are there out there of surly football, baseball or hockey players, where people say "That guy should go get a real job"? Figure skaters give the impression they're walking around saying, "Boy, am I ever lucky." They're great role models.

Then you add the fact that this, as much as—maybe even more than—any other thing that Canadians do in life, we do well consistently. That's a major value for us. Canadians feel good about skating, so they're going to watch it. We've always been made to feel good, from the Don Jacksons and the Jelineks, right through the Magnussens and Orsers to the Brownings and Stojkos.

It's a feel-good thing. It's where we come from. We're only 28 million in population. When there are peace treaty talks or trade talks, we're way at the bottom of the totem pole. But man, get the Zamboni off the ice, put our skates on, and we're up there with everybody. And that, I think, is the real heart of why skating is so popular in Canada and why it's so important to us.

What concerns me is that we—television, the athletes, the sponsors, the ISU, the agents—have a great thing going here. This sport has exploded. In Canada this sport has been mature for a long time. But it's taken off in the States because of the whack in the knee, Fox getting football from CBS and CBS having to find products. So it's exploded in the States, and as with most things, [the States] drags the rest of the world right along with it.

We—and again, this is everybody—have to figure out where we want to go with this, or there is going to be too much skating on, which will lead to confusion among viewers, which will lead to apathy in viewing habits—"I just saw that last week"—which will lead to decline in sponsorship, and now you're into a downward spiral.

I sit here today and there is no real red-light danger signal that the downward spiral is beginning, but I do feel right now there's not a joint strategy for taking this sport to the next level.

I do worry about killing the goose that's laying the golden egg. What we've tried to do is put figure skating shows on the air that have some meaning to them, so that the viewer can look at them and say, "I understand what this means. I understand why this person wants to win."

I think the direction for the future is for the skaters themselves to say, "This thing we love so dearly—we have to be the keepers of the flame on this one." Because they're the ones who would have the power to do so.

JOYCE HISEY

A Lifetime of Service

You don't see Joyce Hisey on television much, except perhaps making the occasional presentation to medal winners at the podium. You don't read much about Joyce Hisey in the newspapers, either. But without Joyce Hisey, and people like her, there could be no major figure skating events, at least not at the amateur level.

At the 1997 Worlds, for instance, not even her closest friends saw much of Hisey. She was tucked into a back room—hunched over a table under an accountant's lamp, poring over figures and contracts and organizational structures—for most of the week.

Hisey is a formidable behind-the-scenes presence at international events, and was so long before 1992, when she became Canada's representative to the International Skating Union, replacing the venerable Don Gilchrist. She and Claire Ferguson, an American, are the only women on the 13-member ISU Executive Council, which spearheads all decisions affecting the future of figure and speed skating in the word. Broadcasters say that Hisey gets things done. "She just says, 'Tell me what you need and we'll get it. Don't worry,'" praises one major network executive.

You might expect that with her longevity in the sport—she was silver medalist in dance at the 1951 Canadian nationals, then arduously wove her way through the tradition-bound judging and technical administration side of the sport— Hisey might be a staunch conservative. Yet she is anything but. She was one of the first upper-level skating volunteers to recognize the potential of catering the sport more to television, and she has been at the forefront of the prize-money revolution in the ISU.

She is accommodating and encouraging, but also unfailingly honest and feisty—she was once torn to shreds in the British press for having the colonial gall to place Torvill and Dean second in a compulsory dance.

She was in the inner circle when the ISU at first decided to ignore the rapid ascendancy of pro skating, then, under Ottavio Cinquanta, quickly put up its dukes.

It took a lot of discussion to try to see where it all fit together—the eligible skater, the ineligible and keeping people in the sport. There's always a vast exodus after an Olympics. And we're going to have it again, at least I think, no matter what prize money we offer. They will move to the other. The pressure's not as great. It's a different kind of pressure, but it's not as great.

I don't think anybody thought that Oksana [Baiul] was going to end up where she is today, a professional. I don't know that Oksana was given a lot of thought by anybody at that time. She was very young, and I don't know what enticed her into that field, why she did leave, other than for the money. I often feel that we don't live in those circumstances she grew up in, we haven't come from that environment, so it's hard to put ourselves in [such a skater's] place.

There certainly were some discussions along the line that we'd lost a great skater, and I think this is where prize money came along. We consciously felt we had to offer these people something to stay. How to get into this field was debated long and hard, and I think some of it is working and some of it isn't.

I think we're wearing our skaters out. They're going everywhere and they're not training. So they come to a major event and perhaps they're not prepared. They're weary. They've competed maybe five or six times in two months. Often you train someone to peak once. It's something that has to be addressed, and so does where the open competitions fit in to it all. Paying a much larger amount for Worlds may be something that has to be addressed, but in order to do that, you have to find more contracts to bring the money in. And if you swamp the market with figure skating, the contracts aren't going to be as lucrative.

I think we certainly all considered very seriously how we could keep things best balanced within our budget, and within the kinds of things we've always done in the ISU.

I would say the door opened with the USFSA and Claire Ferguson spearheading the open competitions. I think they were looking at it from an entertainment point of view and another place where skaters could earn money, but still within eligibility rules.

And at that time, of course, with Kerrigan and all that, the popularity was terrific, and the skaters were going into the professionals.

I don't really know what the answer is. I hear on one side that we're swamping the market and people are getting tired of it. And then all of a sudden there will be one very good competition that everybody enjoys and talks about for a long time.

Where Are We Going? Where Are We Now?   *127*

I think we're trying to keep a control on the content of the events. I know that the Technical Committee is trying to hang on to the judging so that there's credibility to it. I watched a TV program—it was from Florida and I really don't know the name of it. It had Elizabeth Manley, Katarina Witt and Rosalynn Sumners. I've forgotten who-all was there, but with one triple you got a 10.0 and won an event. This makes this whole system, well...rather unusual, I'd have to say. It's ridiculous when you see what we demand from the skaters. And we try to keep the judges trained. And then you come out and you look at this.

I think that our judging system has been tried and true over many years. I think there will always be the moment when something will happen. We have done trial runs of taking the high and low marks out. We've tried that on many occasions, doing the results over again and seeing where that would leave things. Did it make any difference? Does it do this? Does it do that? It really doesn't. I don't know of any system you could put in place that would work better. If you took the high and low marks out, it might solve one problem, but it might create others.

I feel if you're going to make a change—you make haste slowly.

MORRY STILLWELL

It's Big Business Now

The two vocations of Morry Stillwell's life have probably been very helpful with his avocation. Stillwell is a businessman (California Transatlantic Microelectronics) and earlier was involved in flight testing during launch operations at Cape Canaveral. So he brings to the presidency of the USFSA an intimate knowledge of both big business and of things that can take off.

Stillwell became 25th president of the United States Figure Skating Association in May of 1995, and has been involved in the association as athlete (ice dancing), judge (singles and pairs) and administrator. He and his wife, Elda, who is a national-level skating accountant, live in Malibu, California.

I date myself, but I was skating in the 1950s. And up until probably the middle 1980s, if skating was reported at all in the newspapers, it was reported on the society page, along with horse jumping and lawn bowling and things such as that.

Now we've made it onto the sports pages, and some of the sportswriters have become very knowledgeable and recognize it as an athletic sport. Let's face it. It's like running a mile, jumping the hurdles and still looking good.

Certainly in the mainstream, we've come under the microscope. We had over 300 press people at our national championships. We had approximately 200 television people. It became a media event.

[Skating's coming of age] is not reflected in growth of membership as much as it's reflected in who knows about skating. I think television has more to do with that than probably anything else. Over a period of five months, there probably isn't a week where there isn't something on television.

People watch the sport—they begin to get an idea of what it's all about—and when they watch the sport, that's when the young child says, "Let's go try this."

The second thing that's helped in the United States, believe it or not, has nothing to do with figure skating. It's about the explosion in amateur hockey. I come from Los Angeles, and for years we had two or three ice arenas. We've probably got 22 ice surfaces now, mainly servicing youth and adult hockey. But they can't fill up all the time. So what happens? They form a figure skating club.

Canada always had a lot of ice arenas, partly because the provincial governments helped put them together. We don't have that. Most of the arenas in the United States are commercial ventures. For instance, in California, there is a state law that says a government cannot go into any business that has a commercial competitor. So entrepreneurs are building rinks and they're building them in growth areas.

So you have the exposure through television. Our major network is ABC, but there is CBS and Fox, Turner, ESPN. Why are they in it? Money. They love the people who sponsor. Even though total ratings have come down, they love the demographics. The people who watch skating buy. [The networks] charge the highest dollar per 30-second spot of any sport, with the exception of the Super Bowl. It's target marketing.

Even though I knew this was going to be a businesslike job, I never had any concept of how much this was a big business. I spend 20 to 30 hours a week. We have a budget of $10 to 12 million a year, compared with $3 to 4 million 10 years ago.

Where Are We Going? Where Are We Now?   *129*

I'm not worried about the future. Concerned. I'm always concerned. We've got to make sure that we have a continued input of athletes. We're fortunate in the United States that we don't have any government involvement the way other countries do. In the distant past, I think maybe we felt sorry for ourselves because the government didn't support us, but the truth is they don't support us and they don't bother us. So we get to run our own affairs.

As long as we have the continued development of coaching—which is really the heart of it—and the parents can afford to support this expensive sport, and we continue to have the income from the events we run so we can support not only the elite skaters but our novice skaters, I don't have a lot of concerns.

I guess there is some confusion with everything on TV, but I give the public a lot of credit. Part of that confusion [has to do with] the way some people do the commenting during the event. Our scoring system is a hard one to describe. Other sports are easier for the casual observer to understand—"47" wins and "46" doesn't. But I find that although the lay public may be confused, they recognize differences in what is being presented.

You say "There's too much skating" and now you really ring my bell. Wait a minute! How many baseball games do you see? How many basketball games do you see? How many hockey games do you see? How many people are saying that's too much? We're still behind them.

And I don't see anybody saying, "Oh, my God, that's overexposure!"

Ages

OSBORNE COLSON

A Life in Plaid

Now into his eighties, Osborne Colson is still coaching young figure skaters. The gregarious and flamboyant Colson is in Canada's Figure Skating Hall of Fame, and was honored by the ARC Skating Academy in Toronto, one of Canada's high-performance training centers, when the lounge of the arena was named after him in February of 1997. In honor of Colson's trademark haberdashery, the decor is predominantly plaid.

To those who know Colson, it will come as no surprise that even at the age of 12, he was a showman, audaciously sailing his hat into capacity crowds at Maple Leaf Gardens. After a career that included the 1933 junior and 1936 and 1937 senior titles—the only times in 11 years that the legendary Montgomery Wilson was not champion—Colson says, "Life began to look a little more interesting," and he turned professional with Ice Follies. He spent six years with the show, as a solo artist and with Fran Claudet as a featured pair, before turning to coaching.

He has a loyal legion of former students, and at major events is surrounded by an all-ages circle of friends, whom he regales with outrageous tales and observations. It's part of what Barbara Ann Scott calls "The Wonderful World of Os."

My first Worlds was in 1948, coaching Marilyn Take. I won nationals in 1936 and 1937, but they didn't send me to Worlds. If you could find the money, then you could send yourself. If you didn't have the money, you didn't go. In later years, the association found the funds, and if you were a national champion you were sent to Worlds.

I was never bitter about it because I didn't realize just what the event was until I started to get into the teaching racket. And then, when I started taking pupils to the championship, I realized how important it was, what a hoot it was and what I'd missed.

I didn't come from a rich family. Not a poor family, but not a rich one. Some skaters have come from very wealthy families, but I wouldn't say that the good ones have. Barbara Ann's family wasn't wealthy. Friends would just rattle a tin cup up and down the streets in Ottawa, and they got her money.

I trained at the old Toronto Skating Club on Dupont Street, which is now a tennis club. It was an artificial rink, but it didn't have a Zamboni or anything like that. The reason I got going there was that my family had skated before I was even born. My cousin Cecil Smith was second in the world to Sonja Henie. Her sister, Maude Smith, was sixth at Worlds in pairs. My motivation came from those two cousins.

In the 1920s, Karl Schäfer came to the Toronto Skating Club Carnival at Maple Leaf Gardens. They were big, big shows and the Gardens would be packed. We had fantastic lighting and the symphony would play. [The concept] was way ahead of its time. Schäfer had magnificent edges and did good jumps, and he was a great stylist, too. He was Vienna-born, and any of those Viennese skaters had, I guess, an innate [aptitude] for the waltz. He'd do single Axel, double Salchow, double toe, double Lutz and excellent footwork. He had an inside spiral that made him famous. He had a distortion of line—his free leg was bent, where you normally see the free leg straight.

He was a motivator for me. I was a little child star in the show, 12 years old, playing a sailor boy. I'd take my hat off and throw it into the crowd every night.

There weren't many competitions. For the Canadian Championships, you didn't even have to qualify. You just went into them. Then they'd have the North American Championships, and if you won that, you went to Europe and got kind of seeded. The judging, I think, is much better now. Then, you'd almost go by protocol. The dancing still goes a little by protocol, but not the solo skating. It changes almost day to day.

With television now, you find out what other people skate like because you can watch the Europeans and other competitions. But in my day you didn't know what they were doing. And therefore you didn't know what to shoot at. If we'd had television, everyone would have gotten better.

When I first took Marilyn to Europe, for St. Moritz [the 1948 Olympics] the first thing I thought was that I could have been there 12 years ago, loving it. I was feeling a little bit sorry for myself, but I was thrilled to be a coach of the Canadians and to see the athletes marching in. It was a big thing and I felt "Gee, I missed out on this. However, I'm here now."

When you first saw the European skaters you were absolutely mesmerized because they were really good, good, good. The pairs with their death spirals—that's what threw me more than anything. When the Europeans did their death spirals they went so low their heads would touch the ice and the residue from the snow would be on top of the girl's hair. Now you're not supposed to drag the head on the ice. Then, we felt it was a point of balance. But the backs of skaters are much stronger now than then. The physiques and the training of the skaters are much, much improved.

The European singles skaters were similar to ours, although they were much more athletic and the girls were bigger.

We never got to the rink really early in the morning. They were outdoor rinks, so you had to wait until the sun came up. As soon as it was seven o'clock, the sun was over the mountains and you could skate. Barbara would be there with a shovel, taking the snow off the ice. You wouldn't believe it.

One afternoon, we had a delay in the figures competition because of the weather, and then they started to take the snow off the ice, so [movie star] Yvonne de Carlo grabbed a shovel and started to work—in her white mink coat to the ground. She had taken a liking to American skater Peewee [John] Lettengarver and wanted to help get the competition going again.

When they did figures, the officials put oranges on the ice where the bad spots were. They had them for free skating, too, and you had to skate around the things. And you know how in golf the fans come right around the green? It was the same with figures. For a top skater, all the people were circled right around the girl doing the figure, which kept the wind away from her. But if a skater was, say, third in her country, everyone was inside the hotel having a grog, a rum and tea, and the poor kid would be there just standing still in the wind. I opened my coat wide to block the wind for a couple of the lesser skaters because I felt sorry for them.

It's amazing to think that this sport started in those outdoor rinks and is now in the most sophisticated arenas imaginable.

MORRY STILLWELL

Kids Get a Taste

In sport, the future does not necessarily take care of itself. In recent years, American skating has been more focused on planning for that future and less reliant on expecting that its considerable cream will rise to the top. Like any responsible leader of a national sport-governing body, USFSA president Morry Stillwell is well aware that looking ahead to where you will be is probably more important than understanding where you are.

We've introduced a concept called Team 2002, which is our novice people. We obtained a major sponsor, General Motors, and we ran a very large symposium at Nationals telling our new skaters what this is all about.

We took all our novice people when they were through with their events, and had our top judges, some of our top coaches and some athlete representatives explain to them what competition is all about. We even had the kids do some trial judging. And it was quite amazing. They said, "Wow, this is hard." I told them at one point, "I'm sure glad you're not judging me," because they were a lot tougher than we were.

We did this because we think the informed skater is a better skater. Most of the information that floats around the ice arenas is by rumor. So we said, "Wait a minute, let's bring everybody in. Let the top athletes give instructions to the new people. Have them meet the judges, officials, administration. Let them talk to television people, to our sponsors, to our press people."

I'm getting letters from these little kids 9, 10, 11 years old, handwritten, saying that it was wonderful—"We didn't know skating was like this!"

I'm as happy with that part as I am about what happened on the ice at Nationals.

TARA LIPINSKI

My Day

In March of 1997, at Lausanne Switzerland, Tara Lipinski became the youngest World champion in skating history, out-youthing the legendary Sonja Henie by a couple of months. In fact, had the United States not won a power struggle within the International Skating Union to have a "grandfather" clause—a rather strange adjective to describe anything dealing with a 14-year-old—applied to new minimum-age requirements, she would not have even been eligible for the 1997 Worlds.

Although she had hoped only to place in the top 10 at Worlds, and had finished second twice and third once in Grand Prix events, Lipinski had an unbelievable six weeks in February and March of 1997: winning the U.S. title, the Champions Series (Grand Prix) Final and the World Championship. The emer-

gence of the dynamo from Sugarland, Texas, triggered a raging argument over whether figure skating had become like gymnastics: an exercise in ballistics. At four foot eight and 75 pounds, Lipinski looked even younger than her 14 years, but there is no denying her on-ice presence and athletic prowess. She skates with a lighthearted exuberance, has attractive spins, and her low-to-the-ice jumps are a study in speed and rotational technique. She is the only woman to successfully land a triple loop–triple loop combination.

I wake up around 7:15. I go to the rink and warm up and skate at nine o'clock. I do about two and a half hours. I have a lunch break and then I skate for another hour and a half. And then I go home and I have school from three to seven. I'm in grade nine and have three tutors. On Monday and Tuesday tutors come in and teach me algebra and Spanish, and on the last three days I have the other subjects like history and biology.

Then after that, dinner, homework, watch a little TV and go to bed.

I think I'm different because I travel so much and meet so many people from all over, compared with other kids my age. But other than that, you know, I do a sport and that's it. My hobbies? I like to play tennis. I used to have a horse. I like to hang out with my friends on weekends.

Right now the publicity is fine. You work so hard all year, and if you do something great you deserve to be out there. I like it.

I don't think things will change too much [with her victories].

AUDREY THIBAULT

I'm Like the Others

During the gala finale to the 1997 Canadian Championships, an elfin four foot six skater from Drummondville, Quebec, was hoisted into the air by muscular pairs veteran Jean-Michel Bombardier, to the ringing applause of 17,000 spectators.

Audrey Thibault was only 10 years old, and seemed to be oblivious to what was occurring around her. She had finished second in the novice nationals, a relief to her coaches, Annie Barabé and Sophie Richard, who were almost hoping that she would not win the gold medal. They felt that, despite the CFSA's new desire to fast-track promising youngsters, Thibault was too young to advance to junior ranks. (A victory at either novice or junior level means an automatic promotion to the next level.)

Despite her tender years, Thibault has a strong on-ice presence and plays to the audience, but off the ice she is somewhat shy. With the help of Richard, who translated, we extracted Thibault's thoughts on her life and her sport. When she was asked if she would like to be famous as a skater, her answer was a very honest, very 10-year-old, "Maybe."

I started skating when I was three years old and my parents took me to the rink, but I don't remember what I liked about it back then. Now I like everything about it—the stroking, the footwork, the jumps and the spins.

My favorite skater, my hero, is Michelle Kwan. She's young, she's good and she's very artistic.

When I'm on the ice performing, what I think about is that I just want to do a good program. Sometimes I'm a little bit nervous. I think what makes me a good skater is my stroking. I'm doing the double flip, double Lutz, double Axel and a triple Salchow. This time next year I hope to have triple toe and triple loop. I don't know, maybe I'll have them.

I train five days a week. I start in the morning, skating from eight until 10. Sometimes at noon I skate, too. During dinnertime I go to the rink, and then sometimes I have conditioning at night, for my cardio. I jog and I use the conditioning machines at the rink.

I get up at six. I have breakfast and go to the rink at seven and start skating at 7:30 until twenty past nine. At a quarter to 10 I go to school. The first period in the morning, the rest of the class [grade five] has physical education or they go to the library or they go outside, so I'm not missing anything. I'm the only one in my class who is a skater, but I'm not famous in my class.

I have lunch at 12. Sometimes I go back to go skating, and sometimes I have lunch at my place with my younger sister [Catherine, eight]. We cook. And then we go to school from one to four. Then I go back to my place, and go for conditioning at the rink at five. I live about 10 minutes from the rink. And then I sometimes go back on the rink to skate after dinner. Then I go to bed at about 8:30.

For hobbies, I watch TV. My favorite show is *La Petite Vie*, a Quebec soap. It's funny.

I don't think I'm different from the rest of my friends... I'm like the others.

FRANK CARROLL

Work with What You've Got

When he coached Michelle Kwan to the 1996 World Championship, Frank Carroll was in his 33rd year as a coach. So he is well aware that, at different ages, skaters encounter different problems. The duty of recognizing, reorganizing and reconsidering those problems falls to, first, the coach and, second, the choreographer.

After medaling in three U.S. Championships, Carroll joined Ice Follies in 1961 and the coaching ranks in 1964. He has overseen the careers of, among others, Kwan, Linda Fratianne, Mark Cockerell and Fumio Igarashi; coached Tiffany Chin to Junior Worlds; coached Christopher Bowman for 18 years (a challenge all by itself); taught Nicole Bobek (ditto); and trained Todd Sand early in his career.

In February 1997, he addressed the unique challenges of coaching young female elite skaters.

First of all I try to look at her as far as her physical ability and her physical appearance, which I think are two totally different things. I think when you have very young children like Tara Lipinski, they're going to be on top of their athletic thing because they're so small.

Then that changes—the body grows. Then you start to think of how you can work this game to their advantage—like using the body and maybe adjusting the physical ability. I think when girls get to be 16 and 17 and 18 years old in figure skating, a lot of their physicality goes and they have trouble maintaining high efficiency in the really tremendously difficult things.

But there's another part of their skating—the beauty, and the edge work and those things—that they develop. I think it's difficult for the judges to judge it and get a balance between the things they want. Somebody doing less more beautifully and better—is this better than somebody hitting all the triple jumps as a little girl? I think that's sort of what's going on with Tara and Michelle right now.

When Michelle was young and small, I took advantage of doing all the difficult things, bing, bing, bing. We tried to cram the difficult things in and let the artistic go. As time went on and her body changed as she grew older, I had to take advantage of the other aspect.

In 1996, we tried to get into the second mark—the artistic mark, the presentation mark—and tried to improve the overall quality of the program. How did we do that? Good choreographer—brilliant, in fact—better music, concept of costumes. Like sort of working on the visual part of it, which we had ignored up to that point.

There was makeup, but not a lot of makeup. She never wore makeup at school. Chinese girls don't wear makeup when they're young. But then again, as I explained to her parents, Chinese girls if they were in the New York City Ballet and they were 15 years old would wear makeup. She was not going to school when she was in front of 22,000 people—she was doing a performance. They think nothing of spending a few thousand dollars on a fabulous dress. But no makeup?

It wasn't really hard to convince them. I think they knew that their daughter skated probably better than anybody did in Birmingham [at 1995 Worlds] and didn't get the marks. And we were trying to figure out why, so they were willing to agree to [the makeup].

Now, in 1997, I would like to recover from a little disappointment [a second-place finish at Nationals] and see if I can just get the athletic thing going, click, click, click. We've got the visual thing going now—it looks great. It's lovely and beautiful and all that. But now the [question] is, can we get the technical thing going—click, click, click—like when she was 14 and 15 years old?

MICHELLE KWAN

Flying Again

The most valuable experience is the kind you're not aware of while you're accumulating it.

Very few skaters have ever dominated a competitive season the way that Michelle Kwan loomed over the 1995–96 season. At the age of 15, she won all three Champions Series events she entered, captured her first U.S. senior title, was the inaugural Champions Series (now Grand Prix) Final winner and emerged from a brilliant skateoff with defending champion Lu Chen to capture the World Championship. Many observers regarded that night in Edmonton as the greatest head-to-head women's free skate confrontation in the past quarter century, if not of all time.

Kwan was the youngest American champion in more than 30 years, the third-youngest skater ever to win a World title and the youngest American skater to wear a global crown.

However, those "youngest" designations would last only one year. The next season, 14-year-old Tara Lipinski won the national crown, the Grand Prix Final and the World Championship, with Kwan second in all three events. On paper and at the pay window, it was a good season—including three fall international wins—for any skater who hadn't accomplished what Kwan had the previous year.

Kwan's coach, Frank Carroll, berated the media for labeling his skater a "shoo-in" for the national title—"There is no such thing," he said—and he was correct. Kwan struggled through one of the worst performances of her life in the free skate at nationals, admitted to uncertainty as she prepared for the Grand Prix Final and eventually rebounded with a brilliant performance to win the free skate at Worlds. It wasn't enough, because Lipinski was second—two judges ahead of the gritty Irina Slutskaia—in the free skate and that gave her the title.

But Kwan matured more in finishing second than in winning the title the year before, and it shows in her intelligent analysis of the season. She had run headfirst into one of sport's strongest axioms: it is not as difficult to win a title as it is to defend one. She had publicly admitted that she was struggling to regain her aggressiveness and self-confidence, and when she recovered both to deliver that exceptional free skate, she felt as if she, too, had won.

I t was a tough year for me. Not just not winning the nationals and the Worlds, but just as an overall experience. I needed that year...just to wake me up. What I learned was to not take everything for granted. To mentally be tougher, to be stronger. I thought the world was mine. I didn't own it, and I guess I thought I did. I took everything for granted. I was, like, "Oh, this is going to be a piece of cake." I've worked hard, but I have to know that there are other competitors here, too.

I'm so used to being so young, compared with all the other skaters. Now I feel I'm the older one, looking down. I'm "Jeez, I'm getting old." I feel pretty old, compared with Tara or some others. It's a bit awkward now. I used to be the teeny one. You have to know that people are coming up—they're right behind you.

In the [1997] Nationals, I panicked. I didn't really focus on what was going on, what the next thing to do was. I just had this scared look that you shouldn't get when you're performing. I've done that program a million times and I kind of lost it right when I fell on the triple toe–double toe, the second jump. It's a jump that I never miss. It was kind of a shock for me, and I still hadn't gotten to my hardest point. So by then I panicked, kind of got scared. I don't think that had happened to me before, and I wasn't tough enough to overcome the challenges. I was very scared, instead of being determined to do it.

I couldn't believe what I did. I'd never done that in competition, especially at the national championships. During the two or three weeks before the Grand Prix Final, I kind of got myself back together. I was skating better in practices and just having more fun. During Nationals I put so much pressure on myself to do well, instead of just letting myself do it. I put myself in all kinds of situations, and I don't think I want that to happen again. That's how people become stressed out, or they feel so...so captured. I just enjoyed skating a lot more.

At the Grand Prix Final in Hamilton, I thought it was an okay performance, but I knew I could do better. I just kind of took it one step at a time, and tried to improve from those competitions. Hamilton was a baby step from nationals. It was lot better than Nationals, but I just had to be tougher—and I knew that—to get through Worlds.

During the qualification round, I didn't skate well at all. I was skating very well during practice, and I knew I could do it, but I think I just got scared and very chicken. I stopped at that moment and I thought, "If I keep this up, I'm not going to get anywhere. So get this out my head. I've been chicken in Nationals, Grand Prix and now this." And I knew that once I was into the short program, I couldn't be chicken, I'd have to go for all I had. And I think that stuck, that attitude. And that's why I finished strong.

I had trouble with the triple Lutz in the short, but I think that was just a mistake that happens once in a while. I felt really good in the short program, actually. There was just that one slight mistake.

I knew I was fourth, and that if I won the long I still might not win. So I thought, "Okay, this is going to show how tough I am and how I can handle this." So I wanted to put the situation in my hands, and be in control. I felt I did that. I went through it step by step, and it wasn't so rushed. I took it one thing at a time and I didn't let my program go, at any point.

I felt really thrilled. I'd gone through so much. I learned a lot more than I did winning the World Championship. During the year, I thought I wasn't learning anything. I thought I wasn't having a bad year. I kind of ignored every-thing. At the end at the World Championship, though, I learned that I had experienced so much. I noticed. I didn't ignore it.

I learned to have more fun. That's my key thing now—going to the rink with joy, instead of putting myself in situations. A lot of people forget that. People take skating as a job, as something that they're forced to do. Briefly, before the national championships I felt that I *had* to do it. It was as though I forced myself to do it, instead of letting myself go to the rink and have fun, have fun working hard. I don't take it as a job, and that is a good thing, instead of going there and torturing yourself. My body knows how to do it. I just have to let it go. I held myself back for Nationals and Grand Prix and I just couldn't go for it.

I think the experience will help me a lot, preparing myself and attacking, instead of just defending something. I felt that my wings were clipped, that I couldn't fly. That's what I mean by having fun and enjoying what I love doing, and that's skating. I didn't get into the skating world just to win the Olympics or win lots of money. I really just came into skating to have fun, to look at it as a sport, to improve and work hard and see that hard work pay off. I think that's the most solid ground I've ever walked on. It's the best feeling. I just feel com-fortable on the ice.

It felt great to be able to fly again.

TONIA KWIATKOWSKI

Not Finished Yet

When Tonia Kwiatkowski finished second at the 1996 U.S. Championships, she was just shy of her 25th birthday. The other two female singles skaters who quali-fied for the American World team were 13 and 15. Neither Tara Lipinski nor Michelle Kwan had been born when Kwiatkowski started taking lessons 17 years earlier from Carol Heiss-Jenkins, who is still her coach.

When Kwiatkowski had a disastrous 1997 Nationals, finishing sixth—her first time out of the top five since 1990—her place as senior citizen on the U.S. women's team was taken by Nicole Bobek, age 19.

Kwiatkowski, one of the rare elite-level competitors who has also passed high-grade tests—gold dance and bronze pairs—in the testing stream, graduated with a degree in communications and psychology from Baldwin-Wallace College in Cleveland in 1994.

It was mentioned to her that perseverance is a rarity in a sport that has increasingly become the domain of girls, not women.

O h, absolutely. I mean, when you're 12 years old, you can jump like crazy. I think I was very fortunate that my body didn't change too quickly, and when it did, it didn't change that drastically. I was lucky that I stayed pretty tiny.

I was 24 going on 25, and everyone called me "The Old Lady." I don't feel I'm that old. I still enjoy what I'm doing, and as long as I can still do it and do it at the top level, obviously, there's no reason not to. I'd like to stay in until the 1998 Olympics, then do some professional things, because there's a lot of opportunity out there.

I went to college and skated at the same time, and there haven't been many who've done it—Paul Wylie and Debi Thomas, that's about it.

It's a difficult thing to do. Just because of the time factors. I was getting up and going to class, then I'd go and skate for a few hours. I had ballet class once a week for my skating, and I was working out. And when I'd come home after skating, it was, "Okay, I want to eat dinner," and then, "Omigawd, I've got to do a paper."

It was important to me. I had a lot of support from my parents. I had a lot of support from my coaches. My coach, Carol Heiss-Jenkins, was in school when she won the Olympics. Different times, yes, but she had to put a lot of time into her skating, too.

But I had a boyfriend. I did things on the weekends with my friends. I didn't go out on Wednesday or Thursday nights when everyone else did. But it really didn't bother me, because I was doing something I loved and I was getting something that they didn't have. I had the opportunity to travel, to go to international competitions, to be one of the top skaters in my sport. So I mean there is a trade-off. I was doing things they weren't and they were doing things that I wasn't. I had friends and I had fun, but my skating was very important to me.

I have fun outside of skating, and I've met a lot of people outside of skating, which I think is important. Skating isn't going to last forever, so it's nice to know that there are other things that I can do.

I think probably the most important thing is that I love the sport. I love to skate. After the 1994 Nationals I wasn't sure what I was going to do. I really was not going to continue. But Carol and Glynn [Watts] said to me, "Take a couple of months. Think about it."

I was finishing college then, too. And that was when the opportunities were coming along where you could earn some money. That was a big change for me, because for so many years, my parents supported my skating. My dad worked a lot of overtime and my mom would do odd things here and there—she worked for a dressmaker and things like that.

But then it became a completely different time because I could earn money to support my own skating rather than saying, "You're 23. You should get a life and get a job." I mean, this could be my job.

And I still wanted to skate. I didn't feel I was finished yet . . . and I wasn't.

TODD ELDREDGE

You Grow into It

It's surprising how many top names in every branch of the entertainment industry are naturally shy people. In skating, there are a few stars who are born showpeople, but far more commonly, it was something they grew into. The two Brians, Boitano and Orser, are classic examples, as is Ekaterina Gordeeva and even, to some degree, Katarina Witt. Another is World champion Todd Eldredge, a humble East Coaster who early in his career—even during his World bronze medal season of 1991—rarely glanced up into the crowd.

Some skaters undergo an artistic epiphany—Orser had his Pink Panther routine, Boitano his outgoing Sandra Bezic-inspired 1988 Olympic program—that is a clear demarcation point in their creativity learning curve. And it's important to remember that skating is so technically challenging that the athletes have to feel confident with the "tricks" before they can sell the magic.

Then there is the complex process of getting to know yourself.

For Eldredge to find his artistic niche, it was a matter of all three. He used his Charlie Chaplin program of the mid-1990s as a conduit to the performer inside of him, and he had confidence in his jumps and spins.

But, he says, it was the third component—growing up—that made the greatest difference.

*C*harlie Chaplin was definitely something different artistically than I'd ever done. You could say it was a coming-out kind of thing, I guess. But I think it really comes from maturing, getting older, for one thing. And feeling more comfortable skating on the ice. When you do get older, you realize that those people out there are really enjoying what you're doing. You don't have to be shy, just go out there, be yourself, and they'll let you.

When you're first starting out, for any young *guy* in skating it's a lot harder than for females because there's always that air—the homosexual air—about male figure skating. That's always harder on younger kids, and I think that might make them withdraw a little bit. Some kids deal with it fine and some don't. I was kind of somewhere in the middle, I guess. As you start to grow and get older and people start to recognize that you are who you are or whatever, they don't bother you.

It can change just like that—you never know when it's going to happen. It was kind of a gradual thing for me. A lot of it had to do with 1995. I was a little bit more reserved because that was the year I was trying to get back into the scene. I think 1996 really took off as far as my feeling more comfortable and—I don't want to say not caring—but just kind of letting loose. The more confidence you have in your skating and yourself—that really shows on the ice.

And a lot of that comes from maturity.

SHARON ELLER

Youth Isn't Everything

Sharon Eller laughs that turning 30 puts her "halfway to 60," but she's learned that in the skating world, age is nothing to joke about. The less of it the better.

Eller wants to rediscover an opportunity she was never really presented with. At the age of 12, she was declared to have no competitive future and was pointed toward Canada's testing stream. But, despite enjoying her university studies, a stint in a skating show, competitive judging and 12 years of coaching, she could not rid herself of the feeling that there was a place she'd much rather be: competing.

So, at an age when many skaters consider retiring from the rigors of the competitive life, she regained her eligible status and set about the task of finding an ice dance partner. She put the word out in the skating community, arranged interviews with coaches, attended domestic competitions to study the males in partnerships that were about to dissolve. She knew that, even at age 30, she'd be looking at a year or two in junior ranks with a partner several years younger—if she was fortunate enough to find a suitable one. She's come close, but so far she's been unsuccessful in her search. For some of the men, she was an inch too short; others found partners with more competitive experience on their résumés.

She understands the odds she faces, but still suspects she is the victim of age discrimination. No matter that she is athletic, determined—driven, actually—and looks at least eight years younger than she is. What's really being looked at is her birth certificate.

Every year when registration came around, my parents would sit me down very seriously and say, "You know we're working hard to keep you in skating. Your mother [she was a teacher] doesn't have to work, but she does so that we can pay for your skating lessons. Do you really want to do this?" And I'd always say, "Oh, yes, yes, I love it. I love to skate." I always wanted it to continue.

Then they'd say, "Why are you skating?" I had to have a purpose, in their minds. So one year I said to them, "I want to compete," because that's what I always wanted to do. I love dance and I knew I was good at it. But I was shy about being good at it, I think.

So they talked to my coach, because my parents were a bit naive about the skating world, and she said, "No, no. Sharon doesn't have it. She'll never be a competitor. She'll never make it." My parents took her at her word. I think what she was referring to was free skate, and she was right. I'm not a free skater and I don't have that competitive instinct for it. But I have that natural talent for dance and that's what I really wanted to do.

So my parents said, "Your coach doesn't think you're going to make it. You're not going to get to Canadians." They were very gentle about it, and they said, "But you know, you might want to coach someday." So we made the decision that I would continue in the test stream and I would get my qualifications and become a coach. Then I could put back into it what they were putting into it for me.

I was happy with that. I accepted that. Because I didn't know any better.

I continued dancing just because I loved it. When I was 22 or 23 I went to the Cricket Club to skate with Mark Janoschak. He was competing, but I'd just go to skate with him to have someone to skate with. Jacqui [Petr, then his partner] would help with me some things, too.

I also started teaching to help pay for university. So I became what I set out to be, which was a coach, and I enjoyed that. But it wasn't enough.

One day we were skating, and Mark stopped and said, "You could have made it, you know."

It was kind of a kick in the stomach for me. It was a double-edged thing. I could have made it? That was great. Yeah, that was a great compliment. But then it was also . . . I could have *made* it, and I didn't.

I went to Canadians at Hamilton [1993] to watch Jacqui and Mark and there was a team out there that was just awful. I'm not being critical of them. My point is that I felt I was better. If they could make it, I could make it. And I started to take Mark's words to heart.

It was then that I decided this wasn't some big bubble, some unattainable, untouchable bubble, which I'd always thought it was. I could do this. I was close to it and touching it. I had this big "what-if?" hanging over my head, and I couldn't live with the "what-if?"

So since then, I've been determined to do it.

I know I'm old, and I've had lots of tryouts. A few have gone very well, and then they find out how old I am and they say, "Sorry, it's just not going to work," or "We've found someone else."

Mostly it's the coaches. Coaches won't even write your name down if you're over 16. The European coaches, especially the Russian coaches, do think I'm older than most, but they almost prefer older skaters.

One time I had a tryout and called to get directions. I got the coach and he said, "Oh, I'm sorry. I did some research and I found out how old you are, and we're not interested in having a tryout."

So I said, "What does that have to do with it?" And he said, "It's your degree of commitment. Probably at your age, you're going to settle down and you're not going to keep skating." So he just assumed by age, what my degree of commitment or my potential was, and how devoted I was going to be.

To me, it's just the opposite. If somebody at this point wants to do it, they must be something pretty special.

DEBBI WILKES

Too Young to Appreciate It

Outside of Barbara Ann Scott, the most widely recognized female name in Canadian skating just might be Debbi Wilkes.

In her more than 40 years in the sport, she has exerted a strong influence on several aspects of figure skating. She is a successful coach, has written two books, enjoyed a long tenure as color commentator on CTV's major competition coverage and is the featured columnist on the network's wildly popular figure skating site on the Internet.

In 1995, she began her own weekly TV magazine show—Ice Time, named after her first book—on the Women's Television Network. It quickly grew from a cult gem into an integral part of figure skating journalism, and is being considered for syndication in the United States. The format is the perfect vehicle for Wilkes's rare blend of warmth, concern and journalistic directness.

Wilkes has a degree in psychology from York University in Toronto, and a master's in communication from Michigan State that helped point her toward a career in television. But long before she discovered the print and broadcast industries, she had another career, one that flew by so quickly she had retired by the age of 17.

She was a two-time Canadian pairs champion with the late Guy Revell, and in 1964 they won the bronze medal at both the Innsbruck Olympics and the Dortmund Worlds. Later, Olympic silver medalists Marika Kilius and Hans Baumler of West Germany were found to have signed a professional-show contract before the Games and were stripped of their ranking. The Canadians were then awarded the silver medals. Apparently, the Germans have since been reinstated—they are registered in the International Olympic Museum at Lausanne as silver medalists—but no one has ever formally notified Wilkes, and she still has her silver.

Wilkes was six years younger than her partner, and her career serves as a reminder that "Kids at the Worlds" did not begin in the 1990s.

My first Worlds was 1960, when I had just turned 13. I was at least six years younger than everybody else, so I always felt I didn't belong. They were always doing adult things like drinking and...

let's just leave it at "adult things." Not only did I not want to do them, I couldn't understand, at least at that point, why anyone else wanted to, either. So I kind of felt like the odd man out.

I was lucky because my mom always came to the competitions, so I always had a buddy and didn't have to be alone. It was really neat, beginning in 1963 and certainly in 1964, because Petra Burka was on the team, and so was Donnie Knight, so there were starting to be some young kids.

Guy was six years older than me and never tried to make me be older than I was. He always treated me very fairly and was more like a big brother. In those days I was probably closer to him than I was to my own brother, simply because we spent more time together. It was not unusual, if we were guests at a show somewhere, that my dad would give Guy his car. I would have a pillow in the back seat and Guy would drive us there and back. There was never any worry or concern on my parents' part. It was a wonderful relationship we had.

However, when we were on the road and the whole team was there, Guy was with them, not with me, and we would meet up at practice. It was not an issue, but I certainly felt young and inexperienced and naive.

I finished my career when I was 17. We were third on the actual day of competition. The Protopopovs had won and I couldn't imagine ever beating them, they were just so superb. And, you know, I'd had enough.

Guy had been asked to join Capades. They were looking for a partner for Gertie Desjardins, who had partnered Maurice Lafrance as our major competition in Canada.

I was quite anxious to get on with my life away from skating and I wanted to go to school. The CFSA came, through a third party, to my mother and said that if I would continue skating they'd find me another partner, but I wasn't prepared to do that.

I hadn't really been to school since grade seven. I'd go to school, sort of half days, from September to November, maybe, and from then until April I didn't go at all. I had tutors a lot, and then I would cram like crazy in May and June. To a certain extent I felt I'd missed something, but believe me, I was doing what I wanted to do. I didn't regret it. It never felt like a sacrifice.

So, at 17 I went back for my final year of high school, and I nearly failed. I thought it was just a lark. By this time I'd discovered boys and I thought, "Gee, a whole year at school. This is going to be a ball. All I have to do is go to class and this is going to be a snap." I failed at Easter. I wasn't applying myself. I had no commitment anymore, no reason to be organized. I was doing stuff, but doing it badly because I thought all I had to do was go to class. But I really worked from Easter on and got my year.

I have lots of memories of my skating years, but very few of them in comparison with how many there must have been. I started at such an early age—I think I was 11, the first time I was on an international team—that to me it was just a lark. It was something I just kind of thought that everyone did. All the travel, all the wonderful friends you meet—I thought that was just a normal way of living.

The difficult time came after I retired, naturally. Because I was letting the skating friendships slip and I didn't have other friends to take their place. I really didn't have any school friends outside of one girl.

So in letting my skating community slide, there was a huge hole in my life, and I would say for a couple of years I was pretty bitter about the whole thing. I thought it was really unfair how champions were just kind of discarded. I actually thought that people liked me, and it wasn't that way at all. It took me a couple of years to figure out that there is a kind of fickleness in the world, where people like to talk to people they think are famous or important. It really has nothing to do with who you are. And I found that very difficult to handle, somehow.

In that situation you don't really know who your friends are. It's very difficult for skaters, because we start so young. You don't get a chance to learn the kinds of skills you would have developed in a normal school system, under normal adolescent kinds of experiences. What has been your buzz your whole life has been fame and success, and that has become the only thing your appetite will settle for. It's not very real, and it's not a very happy situation in the end.

I really think I was lucky to get out when I was young. I have a hard time when students of mine come to me and say, "I want to be an Olympic champion." I tell them, "I will help you however I can, but be careful what you wish for, because it may come true.

"And it's not what you think it is."

The Ecstasy and the Agony: Winning and Losing

RUDY GALINDO

The "Real-Life" Rudy

Somehow, the United States Figure Skating Championships always seem to find a way to be among the most dramatic sporting events of the year. Whether it's Kerrigan–Harding, the Tara Lipinski triumph, Nicole Bobek or reigning World champions being unable to retain their national crowns, the U.S. nationals are a constantly renewable source of what writers refer to as "good copy."

The "story" of the 1996 nationals was more poignant, and more real, than most. A neutral observer could have been forgiven for asking why Rudy Galindo was still competing, a question Galindo had asked himself. His national ranking had dropped from fifth in 1993 down to eighth in 1995. He had little money for training; his sister Laura was coaching him free; his pairs partner, Kristi Yamaguchi, with whom he had finished fifth in the world, had dropped him in 1991 in order to concentrate on singles; his father had died of a heart attack; his brother and two former coaches had died of AIDS. When possible medalists were discussed, he was not.

As the 1996 Nationals opened, what interest Galindo did stir arose from tangential things. He was one of the few Spanish-Americans in the sport; he had grown up in a tough area; the nationals were in his hometown of San Jose; and in Christine Brennan's recently released book, Inside Edge, *he had willingly revealed that he was a homosexual.*

As the 1996 Nationals closed, the Rudy Galindo story—now a revealing autobiography, Icebreaker—*was being praised as the comeback tale of the decade. He was the new American men's champion, and the new American hero.*

Well, you know it took me a long time [to win]. I went into seniors in 1987, and it took me a lo-o-o-ng time—all the way to 1996. What kept me from doing well was probably just doubting myself and having that voice on my shoulder saying, "You're gonna fall." It probably started when I came down from pairs and tried to adjust to singles. It probably came from everything that was going on in my life, all the bad situations. And once everything was gone, I started believing in myself and telling [the voice] to shut up.

The pain of the bad situations never really goes away, but you just feel better and are content that nobody is suffering, and you go on with your life and concentrate more on your skating.

I asked myself all the time why I was still skating. I had a feeling that people were probably asking that. I thought that maybe one day I could make the World team, and that was how I wanted to end my career. I said to myself that I might as well skate my last Nationals in my hometown because they rarely come to a skater's hometown. I said I'd give it one last try, work very hard, just have fun out there and ignore the judges and all the negativity that goes around. My expectations were to just basically have fun and skate well in front of my home crowd. My friends and family had never seen me skate live. I wanted to go out in style.

When reporters wanted to talk about revealing that I'm gay, it was kind of shocking at first, but I thought, "Oh, I guess I am, and people have to know, and obviously they know now." I talked to Christine about it because I'm proud of myself and proud of who I am. And I have nothing to hide.

I was trying to help other skaters, and people coming out of the closet. A lot of times when people don't come out, they're depressed with their lives. They're so down on themselves because they can't come out, and they're miserable. A lot of people try to commit suicide. I thought maybe I could help in that way, saying that it's okay to come out, in the workplace and to your family, and you can be a better person, too.

Even now, the people in the media keep going on and on about it. But that's what they want—to hear my story. What's that have to do with my skating? I guess it's interesting, but it's all they ask me now. "What about being gay?" "Who's in the closet?" They ask me to reveal people, but I don't.

Even with all the media questions, the week was really fun because I got to stay at home, I got to go to my regular gym, I got to hang out with my friends and go shopping in the malls and stuff.

On the way to the Coliseum for the free skate I went to the cemetery where my dad and my brother are buried. I talked to them, and wanted them to help me do a clean program so I could support my sister and my mom.

I don't remember a thing about the free skate [except] it was so easy…on the jumps the voice wasn't there at all. And then I got off the ice. I was really excited that I'd done a clean program and I couldn't wait to hug my sister. Then the two 6.0s came up, and it was so exciting to see that. Then the computer came up and showed I was first. I jumped right up, but you want to do more. I wanted to jump right out of my skin.

When I went into the corridor I ran into Debi Thomas and Peggy Fleming and they said, "Welcome to your new life! It's not going to be the same."

And I went, "Huh?"

And my new life did begin that minute. Now the media wanted everything out of me. I got to travel and do shows. People recognized me on the streets. I got to make money.

If I looked back, before Nationals I probably thought that right now I'd be coaching kids.

But I'm too busy to look back.

PAUL MARTINI

The Wheels Fell Off

Canada had not won a pairs World Championship since 1962 or an Olympic title since 1960, when Paul Martini and Barbara Underhill entered the 1983–84 season on a tailwind of optimism.

It turned out to be an extraordinary roller-coaster season that ended with one of the most stirring sporting moments in Canadian history. No one who was in the Ottawa Civic Centre that night will ever forget the thunder of that crowd.

But before the peak of Ottawa came the valley of Sarajevo, where Underhill and Martini had to endure the week that almost broke up their partnership. If it had, the skating world would not have seen them go on to become the greatest professional pairs skaters ever.

Like a lot of world-class athletes—golfers are famous for this kind of mental reenactment—you'll notice that Martini changes from the past tense to the present when he puts himself into that very painful, and completely unforgettable, few seconds when their Olympic medal fell out of their hands and slid quickly away from them.

And, given the financial and political factors, can you imagine any world-class skater today deciding to skip the entire fall season?

We were coming off a Worlds in which we finished third, and there'd been a little bit of scuttlebutt that maybe we should have won. For us, it was the first time that we had put together two solid performances, short and long.

We made the decision that we would ride that wave. We would ride that talk that "Oh, the Canadians should have won the World Championship." And we decided not to compete internationally that fall. It was a roll of the dice, but we were confident that we would ride that wave into Canadians and then onto the Olympics, and just be that team that everyone was still saying should have won last year.

And then sort of the wheels fell off.

The preparation through summer and early fall was going fine. Barb was struggling a bit with boots, but you persevere because you figure they'll be fine. And that got compounded the day after the Christmas–New Year's holidays. Throw double Axel and she tears up her ankle.

So now, suddenly we find ourselves in a situation where the first event of the season is to be Canadians, and we're not going.

The throw double Axel was the least consistent of the throws we were doing at the time. And when you've injured yourself on a certain element, that begins to play head games on you every time you do it from then on.

So, Canadians is a pass. There we were, middle of January, trying to get back on the ice as quickly as we could, with our first event of the entire season going to be the Winter Olympic Games.

It was a scary, scary time. But we managed to get ourselves to the point where we still believed we could do it, so off to Sarajevo we went.

We were struggling, and I must say we weren't exactly at the top of our game going in, but knowing or feeling we could kind of pull a rabbit out of a hat, sort of thing.

So now you get to the short program and it's going fairly well. We've executed solidly to the point where we're going into the side-by-side spin and from here on in it shouldn't be a problem.

And then the bottom falls out.

Barbie falls stepping into the spin. I don't see this. I'm spinning and she falls at a point where that moment I'm blindsided. I'm at a point in my rotation where I can't see her anyway. Bang. And you're down. You realize very quickly, very obviously, what happened. You quickly jump into auto-pilot mode. You get up. You finish the program. You do it as best you can.

And then you realize there's something not good here.

Then things go from bad to worse. We were seventh after the short. You know in your head if you're seventh coming out of the short program that unless the entire field has a complete, total disaster you're done. This is the Olympic Games. You're not banking on an event that's going to be full of mistakes. And so you realize the gig is up. Coming into the event as a medalist from the previous World Championship to find yourself in seventh spot! Even the most brilliant performance is not likely to get you back up on the podium.

We had a day off between the short and long. What a thrilling day that was. I can remember feeling, "You know what? Why are we even bothering to do this long program?" That shouldn't be your attitude, but I know for me it certainly was. You sort of feel you want to keep looking on the bright side, on the surface. For your partner's sake, who is feeling worse than you because that's the person responsible for the predicament you're in. But it's tough, because inside of you is one thing, and the façade is another.

You've got to deal with your own demons, but you're certainly sensitive to the other individual's, as well. If you've skated pairs or dance long enough, you've been on that side of the fence before, so you know what it feels like. And you know what you want to hear and what you don't want to hear. I've had more than my fair share of mistakes along the way, so [I] know what it's like to be there. So there is sort of a mutual understanding as to how you're going to deal with the situation.

So now it's the long program. We had trouble with a whole lot of things. I remember the program being two-foot here, step-out there—it was a really lackluster effort. And then just wanting to get out of Sarajevo. But we had to stay to the end.

I remember feeling like a lead stone around the Canadian house where all the other Canadian athletes were in the village. You didn't feel you were the person anyone really wanted to run into. It puts everyone in sort of an awkward situation. You don't know what to say. Should you say something? Should you not say something? You feel, "If I could just get out of here, nobody would have to deal with that. They could just concentrate on their task." Which is what I'd like to think they were all doing anyways, but you still feel that way.

Finally you get to go home and you say to yourself, "Okay, Worlds are in Ottawa in three and a half weeks, or whatever it was, and we've got a lot of work to do." But nothing's clicking. It's a period of time where you thought you could leave [defeat] behind. But it's baggage. And it's a big bag and you're still carrying it around and you don't know what to do with it.

And it almost, I think—I don't think, I *know*—it almost cost us the trip to Worlds.

BARB UNDERHILL

Fate (and Brian) Steps In

In the ensuing years, Barbara Underhill had to brave far more profoundly painful experiences than finishing seventh at an Olympic Games. But at the time, the sense of loss seemed like the worst thing that could ever befall anyone. And the lost medal was not the only thing she stepped onto the plane from Sarajevo without; she and Paul Martini felt they had also lost favor.

Underhill says that skating—particularly her early coach, Anna Forder—has taught her life skills—"about falling down and getting up and doing it again and not giving up"—that have stuck with her to this day.

She needed every one of those life skills—and more than a little fate—to get through those three weeks in 1984 between the desolation of the Olympics and the triumph of the World Championships.

She picks up her partner's story from the trip home from Sarajevo.

I remember getting off the plane in Toronto, coming through the terminal, and there was a huge crowd waiting to greet the Olympians. Brian Orser was right ahead of us and he went first. He had won the silver, and the crowd just went wild as he walked out.

We came next. And the crowd went silent. Just went silent.

It was the worst feeling. Nobody knew what to say to us. Nobody could look at us. I don't know how to describe it. It was just such an awkward, awkward silence, because no one knew how to react.

During those weeks after the Olympics, people would avoid us. They'd see us coming and they'd kind of go the other way. They didn't know what to say. It made [losing] even more difficult, because suddenly we didn't feel the support that we had felt up until that point. We felt even more that we had let everybody down. We also felt that they had given up on us, and that was the hardest thing to take.

So it was really hard to pull ourselves into the rink every day. It was really like pulling teeth going in. We were communicating very poorly because we were hurting so badly. We couldn't talk about it. We were young, but it's like anybody who deals with something truly devastating—you grieve in different ways. We were having a really hard time communicating and getting through it.

To make matters worse, we were coming to the rink and hoping that something magical was going to happen and that suddenly everything was going to be okay.

[Skating] wasn't natural for me anymore. I had been struggling all season. I had torn ligaments—we hadn't competed all season. It wasn't natural—it wasn't fun. It was work. I remember Louis [Stong, coach] taking me to a psychologist to see if it was something in my head that I couldn't deal with. I knew that that wasn't the problem, but I was willing to do anything. I think he thought it was confidence or that I didn't believe that I could do it, but physically, there was something wrong. I'd been struggling with boots all season, and when we got back I decided to go into a new pair right away. We only had about three and a half weeks [to Worlds], so it was a big move to go to a new pair of boots with so little time.

I went into the new skates, and they were worse than what I was wearing. When we took a close look, they were totally out of kilter, so they helped to strip my confidence even more. I tried another pair of boots, which also didn't work, so I was really struggling.

There was one week before the Worlds, and we had to make a decision. Neither of us wanted to go there and embarrass ourselves in front of a home crowd in Ottawa. But at the same time we didn't want to give up, because this was going to be our last chance.

So the fateful day at the rink, it just all came to a head. We weren't talking. I went out to get on the ice and I noticed that Paul was sitting in the lounge and he was just staring out blankly at the ice. He didn't even have his skates on.

It looked to me like he had given up.

Louis called us into his office with Sandra [Bezic, choreographer] and he said, "Why don't we just call it quits right now? There's no point in embarrassing ourselves."

As he was picking up the phone to call David Dore [at the CFSA], I left the office—I just couldn't take it anymore. Brian Orser was sitting on a bench.

He just happened to be skating at the Granite that day. I sat down and started crying, hard, on his shoulder. "There's nothing else we can do. We're not going to go to Worlds."

He said, "Well, why don't you try last year's boots? They worked last year." I said, "Well, I guess it couldn't hurt to try." By coincidence—or fate—the skates that I'd worn the previous year were in the trunk of my car in the parking lot. I took them up and told Paul I was going to give it a try. He put my new blades on the old boots.

I laced them up, and within five minutes I knew that that had been the problem. I just started to fly around the rink. I stayed at the rink until midnight that night and we skated a clean program.

Every day we came into the rink [to practice] we skated flawlessly. We were on such a high...we couldn't make a mistake. It was unbelievable. When people saw me flying around the rink, they said, "Is this the same skater we saw here a couple of hours ago?" It just shows you how important it is that your skates be just really, really right.

We arrived in Ottawa on such a high and just flew through the week. We just couldn't make a mistake.

We were second after the short, to Valova and Vasiliev, who had won the Olympics. We drew second last for the long. The East Germans were last, but at that point they weren't a real consideration.

I have never been so confident in my entire career. I didn't let anything into my consciousness other than the job that I had to do. I could focus so clearly on what I had to do.

When I watch that program today, I can remember exactly what was going through my head during the program. I have never had that kind of clarity during a performance. It was so easy and so focused.

The last really difficult trick in the program was the throw double Axel, and at that point we knew we were almost there. But it had happened so often where we almost there and boom, we go down, so we were so determined to keep that focus.

There's a moment that I see, every time I watch the program, where it's about 30 seconds to the end and I'm coming down from a lift. My head flies up and I look into the audience for the first time and I see people on their feet. I don't know how long they'd been there, but I didn't notice them until that moment. It was the first moment I allowed myself to look out and see the people. It was an incredible moment—I can't even describe it. Even now when I watch it—and how many years later is it?—I still get overwhelmed by the feeling in the crowd.

Sandra says that she was jumping up and down and screaming, "Keep thinking, keep thinking!" because so many times we'd done something stupid near the end.

It just brings it all back when I watch it.

When we came off the ice, it was bedlam. It took absolutely forever to get the marks. Apparently, Johnny Esaw had jumped up, [accidentally] pulling the plug from the computer, and the computer went down. But it was kind of neat, because we had that moment together, just the four of us, to really savor it. Watching it, I can see my lips moving and [me asking] Sandra, "Did we do it?"

Then the marks came up and we knew we had.

It was within a thread of not happening. If the skates had not been in the car, I might not have pursued [going to Worlds].

I believe that things are meant to happen. Too many things have happened to me in life not to believe that. That day there was a reason the skates were in the car, and there was a reason Brian Orser was in the rink. Had he not [suggested my old skates] to me, I wouldn't have thought of it. No one would have.

I think if it wasn't for those Worlds, we probably wouldn't have had the leverage to do what we did in pros. We had a huge amount of momentum going into the pro circuit. We might not have had a chance to compete at the World Pros had we not won. I think competing year after year in the World Pros was what kept us moving forward, breaking new ground.

And had we not skated at those World Pro events, I don't know if we ever would have come up with *When a Man Loves a Woman* or *Unchained Melody*, or any of those.

It was fate.

MICHEL BRUNET

Lost in the Political Shuffle

Michel Brunet is never going to be a World ice dance champion. He knows that. But he'd also like to know where a different approach to dance judging would place him. A North American team in a European discipline, Brunet and his

*partner, Chantal Lefebvre, finished 20th in their second year at Worlds. They
had been 15th in their debut and hoped to rise, not fall.*

*It's not the standing that drives Brunet crazy so much as the feeling that there
is nothing he can do about it. That sense of helplessness is common to ice dancers.
Brunet, at least, has the courage to speak out about it.*

*There were minor flip-flops in the middle dancers, but among the top 15 cou-
ples at the 1997 Worlds, there was only one change from the standings between
the first compulsory dance and the final standings. The 11th-place team dropped
to 13th, slightly shifting three midpack teams. In ice dancing, that's called progressive thinking.*

*You can hear the pain in Brunet's voice, and you wonder how many other
good athletes the sport is in danger of losing.*

Right now, it's a little too late for me to change. But if I had to redo it,
I wouldn't be an ice dancer. I wouldn't even be in the sport. I'd be a
hockey player.

When I was 17 I had a chance to choose hockey or figure skating. I was
playing double-A hockey and my cousin was coaching and said, "You have the
future of being a hockey player." But at that time, too, my mom was supporting me on her own because my dad had passed away when I was 10. I said, "I
have to make a choice," and the choice was definitely going to be in my mom's
favor because she was always with my sister at skating. I said, "I'll make it easy
for you. I'll figure-skate."

But if I had a chance to do it again, I wouldn't do it. Because you get to a certain level and you don't control your own destiny, even in pairs, even in singles.
It's getting to a point where they could send you a fax and tell you what the
results are. Because no matter what you look like, [the judges] are going to
push who they want.

We were 15th [in 1996], knowing that we could slip a couple of spots [in
1997] because a couple of couples came back who were in front of us. But
[the judges] took the bull by the horns and said, "Listen, you're getting
buried. No matter what you say, no matter what you skate, you're going
down." I was talking to the team leader and I said, "If they had told me at the
start of the week that everything I did here would end up being for nothing,
I would have stayed home."

I think what is hard to understand is that it just doesn't come from you. It's
hard to understand, at one point, that it's not based on what you do but who

you know. You know what I'm saying? And it's getting worse and worse and worse.

You accept criticism. As an athlete, you have to accept criticism, especially when other people control your destiny. You do listen to people. You take some—you leave some. But you don't know anymore who to believe—who's right, who's wrong. You get nine people on the panel, and for some reason you get the Canadian judge, who is pushing our country, getting in deep shit. Well, how come the Russians, how come the Bulgarians, how come everybody else is not getting in deep shit? Because they're all sticking together. That's our sport right now. Our sport right now is not fair because all of the new countries coming in—Kazakhstan, Ukraine—you get all the former Russian countries. You go down the list, you get basically a [former Soviet] skater in each pair.

You can't explain what's going on to us. Because of the standings, nobody cares. We're not demanding to be 15th just because we were 15th last year. You should come in as nobody. When you get on the ice, that's where you're judged. But not having the triple Axel, and not having this, this, this, that the singles do, it makes it hard on the judges. I totally understand that. I totally understand why they have to slot us in groups.

But I think it's bad. You should see the bullshit that goes around, and I'm tired of that. Why? Because they don't judge you, they judge who the coach is. The Israelis who finished ahead of us should never have been there, but they have the coach, Linichuk. Shae and Vic should have been second at Lausanne for what they did. And you look at the other guys, where they say, "Okay, we'll go buy the judges." And you can write that. I don't give a shit.

And judges threaten. They say to other judges, "If you don't do this, then you're not going to get that."

I think ice dancers are the toughest mentally, because they keep getting slapped and slapped and then they have to keep getting back up.

JASON DUNGJEN

A Long Time Coming

Jason Dungjen was four months past his 29th birthday when he finally won his first U.S. senior pairs championship. He and his partner, Kyoko Ina, had been second three successive years, but at Nashville in 1997, they won both the short and long programs to capture the title. They headed to Worlds with confidence and finished fourth, to continue a steady rise from 12th in 1994.

Dungjen didn't start figure skating until the relatively late age of 11, and then only to improve his hockey skills. He won a silver medal at the World Junior Championships with his sister Susan, quit skating for a while, then returned with Paula Visingardi. After one year with Karen Courtland, he teamed up with Ina in 1991.

The 1996–97 season was a bittersweet one for them because Judy Burrows, wife of their coach, Peter Burrows, died just a week and a half before the nationals.

It does seem long and it doesn't seem long. Let's see, how long have I been doing this? Forever. I think since 1980. How it doesn't seem long is that I still have so much to do and to learn. It's a sport that you can always improve in. Even when you start to lose the tricks, some of the elements, you can still improve. How it does seem long is the physical—the wear and tear on the body. Certain parts of the body are stiff and sore. I don't know if it's from 18 years on the ice or I'm just getting older.

Our first year as a team, we were happy just to make the Olympic team. That in itself was a big boost for us. Then in 1995, we just came in hoping to skate well, and we did. Our goals were more a top-10 finish at Worlds, which we received.

But by 1996 we started to set a goal of winning a national championship because we thought that two years being second place was long enough. I think it's about mind-set. We felt we had improved enough to win. We came close, but unfortunately didn't quite get it.

Then in 1997 our mind-set changed. It's really hard to explain what happened, but we just got to a point where all we would concentrate on, Kyoko and I, was what it would take to make us a better team. Every day we'd come in and work on the little things. We'd sit down and say, "I'm looking here. Where are you looking?" or "My foot only goes to here. Try and match it." We'd have an arm movement and maybe it would be off because my upper body isn't quite as flexible as hers. So she can move her arm maybe 45 degrees behind her, where mine can only go 30 degrees. So we'd work on those little details that, when you watch skaters, really make the difference between those who win and those who don't.

When the two of you, you and your partner, start to really grab on to the same goal, and you really start to work together, is when things really take off. I think for us it started in 1995–96 but it really took hold in 1996–97. When we stepped on the ice in Nashville, we skated as though we wanted to win.

Basically our mind-set this year was just to take care of ourselves at Nationals. To go out there and skate the way we can skate. And to show everybody that we are as good as anybody else.

We had to wait for Jenni and Todd to skate before we knew we won. Peter and I were watching on the monitor. The marks were so close nobody knew what was going on. I'm looking at the monitor and I see the screen blink, and that means the new marks have been put in. I couldn't figure it out because we still had 1–1 next to us. So I thought, "Maybe it was just a power surge." Then I saw Jenni and Todd underneath us and I just looked at Peter and said, "*We won!?*" Then I went yelling into the dressing room to Kyoko.

The first feeling was relief…and then mostly it was elation after that.

Judy died one year to the day after the diagnosis. We'd found out about the diagnosis a couple of weeks after Nationals the year before. So all year it was really hard because Peter was torn between us and Judy, of course. So he couldn't travel with us. I think that also made Kyoko and I really work together as a team and to get our mind-set. We realized there was a lot going on, and it helped us focus on what we needed to do. And we realized that life can be really short—if you've got the shot you'd better take it.

Judy was one of our greatest fans. She always felt that we could be national champions. I wish she could have been there in person to see us on the podium. But I know that she was there.

KURT BROWNING

The Calm of Winning

There were some times during his four World Championship years that Kurt Browning was not the best skater in the event. But he was always the best competitor. By far.

Browning had an eye for the prize that the other men skaters of his era could only envy. He just had a better handle on how sports are played, and knew that rising to the occasion is the single greatest factor in making a superior athlete.

At Paris (1989), Halifax (1990) and Munich (1991), Browning found a different route, and motivation, to the top of the podium. The good athletes win when they should; the great ones win when somebody else should.

"And how you win is great," Browning says. "But how you lose is so important."

He didn't have a lot of experience with the latter from 1989–91. He felt he was meant to win.

After the quad I landed at Canadians in the first 30 seconds of the program, I knew I was going to win Worlds at Paris. Call that being young and cocky and being ignorant of the fact that Fadeev, Petrenko, Chris Bowman should all win before me. When I hit that one jump, it was, "Screw this, let's go to Worlds." The rest of the program was good, but I was immediately at Worlds. So, I went to Worlds to win.

My coach was telling the press, "He's not going to win," but as soon as I finished fifth in figures I said, "No, no, we could win."

I finished my long early, and I remember sitting there with Michael [Jiranek] and people would skate and their marks were not as good as mine. And we were getting quieter and quieter and just going, "Is this really going to happen?" And every time someone would skate, in my mind I'd be going, "That wasn't as good as me—I'm pretty sure of it. But there's no way they're going to give him worse marks than I got." And then they would. Sitting there watching four skaters, and all of them coming second to me—it was like a dream.

Then Halifax was really hard work. So many distractions and so much pressure. The second one is always hard. I had sore toes, and they were really bothering me. The quintessential moment that year was doubling the second triple Axel in the short, then throwing it in at the end, instead of the double, to save the program. A lot of skaters can't do that. Eldredge can do it. Elvis can do it.

Winning is amazing, because you can usually go back and find one moment—like the TSN Play of the Game—where you say, "That's where I won it." [Of course,] you can also go back and say, "That's where I lost it."

In Munich, I won it before I got on the plane. I just knew that I was skating as good as I've ever skated in my life. My goal was, whatever Victor [Petrenko] does, I'll do one more. That was why there were three triple–triples. I was so cocky and high on myself that I believed I could do it. I used to get like a fighter.

When I win, it's calm. When I lose, there's a turmoil of emotions. Why did you let that happen? What could have been? Who'd you let down? I feel like shit. I wish I could do it again. There are all these things going through your head.

But when you win, it gets quiet and you just sort of wait for nice things to happen. Because you've got nothing left to do except sit back and enjoy.

You can have that feeling almost every night on a show. It's amazing how upset you can get in a 63-night tour when the 48th night doesn't go well. It's really intertwined with our sport...it's our soul and our emotions.

It's really scary sometimes that a pair of blades and an Achilles' tendon can screw up how I feel about myself as a person. But I think that's how deeply we're tied up with what we do.

LYNN NIGHTINGALE

"Fall. Fall. Fall. Fall."

Lynn Nightingale won four successive Canadian championships—without the aid of the technique she describes here. She climbed as high as sixth in the world, before turning to a successful professional career in 1977 as a soloist with Ice Capades. She now teaches skating and works on the production staff for CTV's skating telecasts.

Very few people in the sport have ever combined a sense of humor and sense of adventure the way Nightingale always has. Here, she reveals both as she recalls her attempt—ultimately successful, it would appear—to influence the outcome of a competition in a rather unorthodox manner. And if most athletes were honest with themselves, they'd admit that at one point in their lives they, too, had hoped their opponents would fail.

Incidentally, Nightingale did win the event.

It was the first Skate Canada, in 1973, and the previous year was my first Worlds and I'd done quite well—15th in figures, third in the short program, fourth in the long program. And when I went to Calgary I was expected to win the competition. I think there were maybe 10 or 11 in the competition, and I came seventh or eighth in figures.

The next day I got up and I read, LYNN NIGHTINGALE A DISAPPOINTING SEV-ENTH in big, big, bold print. And I almost had a heart attack, because it hurt my feelings. The word "disappointing." Even with your parents, they can be angry with you, they can be pissed off with you, but when they are "disappointed" it's a much more hurting thing. So that word, specifically, hurt my feelings and I felt bad.

I was in the first group for the short program. I skated very well, I did what I could do, then I got off the ice. And I said, "Now, how am I going to make it all the way up to first?" So I took my skates off, went into the dressing room, and since I'd done all I could do, I thought, "I'm going to need a little help."

[The competition] was in the old Calgary Corral. I climbed to the very, very top row. The last group was warming up, and as each skater came out, I put a hex on them. And every single skater fell at least once or twice.

It was terrible. [I thought,] "Not only am I skater, I'm a witch!" I would say, "Fall. Fall. Fall. Fall." And they Fell. Fell. Fell. Fell. So I won the short program. I'm not sure how far I moved up—I was seventh or eighth and I moved up to either second or third.

Afterward I felt really bad, because I thought that I really had had something to do with it. Because every time I said, "Fall!" *Splat.* "Fall!" *Splat.*

The thing I learned from all of that is you don't want to be the best of a bad lot—you want to be the best of a good lot. And to win because everybody else fell down certainly isn't much of an accomplishment.

After that I [decided], "Skate for me, and whatever happens, happens." And if you're happy with what you've done, then it doesn't matter what the press says, it doesn't matter what your friends say, it doesn't matter about anything. You can only do what you can do.

BRIAN BOITANO

You Don't Know What to Say

What many fans don't know is that skaters share the same dressing room during a competition. It was there that Brian Boitano and Brian Orser first crossed paths moments after the Battle of the Brians had been waged.

The difference between winning and not winning was right there, contained within those four walls, as they looked at each other.

Brian and I weren't really that close before the Olympics. Everyone thought we were friends, but we were very competitive. At times I felt that Brian didn't treat me in the best way, how I deserved to be treated as a competitor. At times, I didn't feel that he would have considered me in the same league.

That's why I treated him so well after I won the Olympics. I wanted to treat him the way I would have liked to be treated.

After I skated, I said, "I skated my best," put on my earphones and went in the dressing room. [I was] listening to a tape timed for five minutes. It was Brian's turn to skate. I never watch anyone else, even after I skate. And when I took off my earphones, all I heard was his very last mark...and what was his very last mark that night? Six-point-oh. That's all I heard. I went, "Oh, well, I lost," and gave myself a pep talk in the dressing room. I thought, "It's okay, I'll do four more years, dah, dah, dah. I'm proud of myself. It's okay to be second."

Then Brian walked in the dressing room and I'll never forget it. He was glazed. He ran his hand through his hair slowly. And he didn't even see me sitting there. His hand went right down his face and he just dropped his flowers and went right into the bathroom. I was, like, "What is going on?" Then Peter Jensen [Canadian sports psychologist] followed him in there and they stayed in there quite a long time. In the meantime, someone said, "You're in first," and I said, "That's impossible. He got a 6.0." But they said, "That was his only six." Victor [Petrenko] still had to skate, and I knew that could change ordinals, so I didn't celebrate or anything.

Then Brian came out and he was so glazed over, and I said, "You know, we've been through a lot. This has been so hard and I don't know what to say."

And I think because of that moment Brian and I are better friends. We went through something together that nobody can experience. The Battle of the Brians is something that only a Brian can know [about]. I think that we wouldn't have been friends the other way around. I still have so much respect for him and what we went through, and I'm so thankful that I won the Olympics. I'm so thankful.

Even when I stepped down off my stand to congratulate him that night before the national anthem was played, I just wanted to make him to feel better. I didn't want him to feel bad.

Brian and I pushed each other tremendously. We made each other. We're the reasons we did triple Axels in the short program. It was just digging and digging and digging. You have to have that. That's what sport is all about.

Brian was great that night—he made one little teeny mistake. I have a lot of respect for him, having to skate after me, because a part of him knew how I skated. So it all came down to him, and I think Brian never got his due from the Canadians for how great a competitor he was.

The Heart (and Art) of the Matter

LORI NICHOL

Apples and Oranges

Is it possible to teach an appreciation of art? Can you take a 50-year-old judge who grew up behind the Iron Curtain and make that judge understand exactly what a 15-year-old skater is trying to portray with her alternative-rock program?

To Lori Nichol, the answer to both questions is yes. She and her friend Ann Shelter are designing ISU seminars meant to help judges "further develop a profound sense of aesthetics."

Nichol is in constant international demand as a choreographer, and her programs were credited with helping Michelle Kwan shed her little-girl image for the mature look that carried her to the 1996 World title.

Although Nichol was born in Canada, she grew up in the States—Philadelphia, then Colorado—but she returned to her native country when she married a Canadian. She had always wanted to take lessons from Frank Carroll in California, yet "it just never came about." So when the opportunity arose for her to take 10 Canadian students to California to work with Carroll she jumped at it. The two hit it off philosophically, and a few months later Carroll called to ask Nichol to choreograph a tiny girl who could do triple Lutzes and might just have a future.

"And it was Michelle," Nichol says with a smile.

Kwan certainly did have a future, and Nichol thinks skating does, too. A broader-based future, perhaps, than its aggrandized present. But only if it recognizes what it can be: an art form that embraces many approaches and styles; that can expand as the general world of art expands. That recognizes the inherent values of, for example, both classical music and punk rock, 20th-century Western themes and 12th-century stories from the Far East.

Nichol will not be seduced by the safety-net theory that you cannot compare apples and oranges.

I can compare apples and oranges, and I don't know why skating can't do the same thing. If the apple is all fiber-y and doesn't have much juice and it's warm and wrinkly, it's obviously not nearly as good as that wonderful fresh piece of orange that sprays when you open it, it has so much juice. Those things can be compared, so to me [saying they couldn't] felt like kind of a cop-out, so let's think about it a little bit.

Can you imagine having to evaluate [the differences]? The judges have a job that you couldn't pay me a million dollars to do, it's so difficult. Think about how many skaters there are, all their different personalities, all the different choreographers and ballet trainers they're working with, and dance trainers and jazz trainers and rap trainers. There are so many opinions out there that you have to have as broad a perspective as possible.

Part of the seminar focuses on [a cultural gap]. We'll take a contemporary painting—say, something like a Monet, which is very clear in what it is about. And using the same eight components in the presentation marks of skating, we'll try to evaluate the work of art.

The ISU—Sally Stapleford, in particular—is working very hard to educate the judges much further. The big thing is to really educate [them on] what the presentation mark is. To study the presentation aspect just as much as, in the last several years, technical has been studied. Through that, only great things can come, because the more judges know, the higher their expectations are going to be. Skaters are going to have to rise to those expectations, and I would hope that everything would snowball.

These judges are working very hard to discover what art is and to define it, and that's a much harder job than defining what the technical is.

Can I define art? It's something that makes you think or feel, see the world in a new light, inspire you. It can be many things.

An artistic figure skater is someone who truly uses the blade-and-ice relationship, who has great body lines and flexibility, who has a great diversity of steps and movements, who is not afraid to skate to music that is not typical music heard in skating rinks, who is willing to open up and be sensitive enough to be an artist. And that is a big risk. To go out there in front of millions of people and do something that you love and believe strongly in and maybe push the envelope a little bit—that takes courage.

The notion before was that the first stage was [to] get the technical aspect, then add the artistry. But now I think people are [wondering], why can't you be working on the technical moves in order to build upon the artistry later? You can't just go out there and paint a picture. You first have to have the tools. You have to know how to hold the paintbrush.

I think the technical mark, understandably, has been given the predominant study and thought. It's probably easier to understand and easier to assess.

Because I was studying it all day every day, I was getting bored with doing

Romeo and Juliet, [with doing] the same kind of pieces over and over. I thought, "Why does skating always have to have the same music? Why does it have to have a highlight here and then a little slow part to show that you can calm down and be pretty, [before you] go like gangbusters again? And why does there have to be such a distinction between professional, or ineligible, skating and eligible skating?"

[Skating artistry] is about getting the music and the skater and the medium of ice to come together and look as if it's one, and entirely meant to be. The skater almost creates the music through the movement. [Skating artistry] is about giving back the love of the sport, as opposed to the tension we've all seen over the last several years [from] trying to do the tricks. And now more and more people are doing the same big tricks, so it's a great time. I don't think we were maybe ready before. Listening to the public, and the coaches, and the commentators and choreographers, I think everyone is really ready.

I'm grateful I live in an era when someone like Sally Stapleford says, "Let's do it." The audience is so knowledgeable now that we need to do this if we're going to keep them interested.

USCHI KESZLER

Boats and Water

Philadelphia-based Uschi Keszler is fiercely protective of any skater who comes under her choreographic care. An intense student of the related, but distinct, themes of motion and movement, she helped transform Brian Orser from a technical skater into an artist, and feels that the same alchemy has been at work with Elvis Stojko.

But, like Stojko, she feels he doesn't get enough respect for his interpretative work.

Artistry is a very unusual thing in skating, and where I find the problem is that people look at the body, which is like watching the painter instead of the painting.

With Elvis, if you stand back a little bit you see the influence he has on space and how he shapes [it] ... the picture that he creates. If you just look at his body, you miss the whole thing.

It's not the body, but the movement of the body. If you look at just a boat, you don't realize the effect it has on water. You have to look at the whole thing.

CHRISTOPHER DEAN

A Process of Evolution

To borrow and bend a little Shakespeare, some men are born artists, some achieve artistry and some have artistry thrust upon them.

Christopher Dean is likely a combination of all three, although he says he was born more of an athlete than an artist and that the pursuit of becoming a better ice dancer released the creativity in him.

And there have been no better ice dancers than he and Jayne Torvill. During their amateur careers—in the first cycle; they briefly redescended from the pros for another Olympic run 10 years later—they amassed 136 perfect scores of 6.0, a whopping 29 of those coming in their farewell appearances at the 1984 Worlds in Ottawa.

They won four World Championships and an Olympic title, but each event was more coronation than competition. They were so far ahead of the pack that the battle was always for the other two medals. The real challenge they faced every year was, could they top themselves?

And they always did. Bolero, *their exit vehicle in 1984, was the crowning achievement of their amateur careers. Torvill and Dean pioneered the concept of single-theme programs with their* Mack and Mabel *routine of 1981–82, a demarcation point for modern skating artistry.*

Released from the bondage of amateur rules—which they had broken, or at least stretched beyond recognition, anyway—they became even more creative in their pro career. Missing, *which Dean designed for their Russian All-Stars Tour, became the Duchesnays' signature piece, and one of the most important ice dance programs of the post-Torvill and Dean era.*

When I was young, I was more athletic than anything...climbing trees, doing gymnastics, running faster, jumping higher. More a competitive, I suppose, than an artistic bent.

I started skating when I was 10. As you progress, obviously you try to get better and develop, and that process has an effect. I think the difference between skating and, let's say, dance is that people go into dance already with an artistic bent. They look at the aesthetics of what their body's doing and they're taught that from the beginning. Whereas I think when you go into skating, you go into it from an athletic point of view, which is a physical aspect. It's about jumping higher or going faster or, if it's hockey, it's about aggression.

I was always in ice dance. I never did singles skating or pairs. So I suppose, to a degree, that that athleticism wasn't as forceful as it would have been doing singles because of the power [singles] required. I was more into the movement on the ice, and just through that process of dance, you become more aware of what your body is doing. And then you want to be in control of your body. And then you want your body to talk.

It's a progression. And eventually—without wanting to get too pretentious about it—that process, when you put it all together, becomes a language. It is a form of expression, and it happens to be on ice. When you get to a certain point you go beyond the athleticism of it to the expression of it, and I think that's what we had.

When we were working together choreographically in the earlier years, it was kind of a process of trial and error. We didn't work with a coach who put steps together for us. Back then, we didn't call it choreography—we called it putting together the routine. Janet Sawbridge [coach] would say, "Well, you make it up and I'll look at it afterward and decide what I like and don't like." She encouraged us to think for ourselves, discover our likes and dislikes. We'd experiment to find new things, and going down that road made us think for ourselves, and I think that was part of our development. At an early stage we developed our ability to choreograph things ourselves. We look at some of the earlier things we did and we cringe, but that was part of the evolution.

Obviously, *Bolero* stands out, but I think the process of getting to *Bolero*, each one—*Mack and Mabel*, *Barnum*—had its own flavor and showed a progression. Afterward, when we turned professional, we had an open door to all things, and not just a competitive routine. We weren't restricted by subject matter, length of time, trying to establish something. We enjoy that freedom far more than "The maximum is four minutes. You can't do this and you can't do that, but you have to include this." It was so defined that it was essentially quite narrow.

The worst part of the process is the beginning. It's like a writer with a blank page—[coming up with] the opening line, the germ of what it's about. The same process with a routine—it's that germ, that originality, that first step, that's the hardest.

You don't want to be repetitive. People will say about skaters, "That's their style." Well, I hope our style isn't necessarily "Well, that's obviously them." We've tried to jump around. *Missing* was one of our more thoughtful routines. We did another piece called *Encounter*, where we wore gray, about two people coming together. Then we did a violent sort of piece to *Revolution*, [where we're] sort of abusive to each other. We've done comedy on the ice. We want to go all over the place. We do a piece to the Bach sixth suite, the cello suite, that when you first hear it, it can put you off. But the more you hear it, the more beautiful it becomes.

When we conceive of a piece, we don't really see steps, more of a mood. A feeling. Light-dark, or bright and sharp, or smooth. Once we've choreographed it from A to B, it's more a question of how it takes us along, why we're doing something, why something leads to something else. It becomes a progression of dialogue. We can say, "Where is this coming from? Why is this there?" And that can be quite narrative, sometimes. On the other hand, it can be very much abstract. A piece that has a blues-jazz feel—it's about movement that comes from somewhere. So we try to make it look organic, from the ice through to our bodies, just very loose and throwaway.

Our skating is for us. Obviously, we like to be liked. The body of work we've done over the years is huge and it's very diverse. And that's what we're most happy about.

TOLLER CRANSTON

The Two Crimes of Art

It is impossible to have a discussion about skating and art and not consult Toller Cranston, the man who drew the concepts closer together than anyone this century. With his artistic temperament, legs that could stretch to impossible lengths and directions, his penchant for the unusual and his consuming desire to be watched, Cranston was, and still is, passion on ice. A balletic pas de un.

He not only knows what he likes, he knows art.

*A*rt, for most people, is a word that is either intimidating or brittle. [Some athletes say,] "I'm a sportsman, but I'm not an artist, and I don't know anything about that." That's not true. Art is simply another reservoir, another pool, another level above the technique. Scott Hamilton is a great artist. Kurt Browning is a great artist. Laurent Tobel is a great artist. Gary Beacom is a great artist. And each paints with different colors, or presents himself differently.

What [their artistry] is, is the intelligence of the human mind that creeps into their technical abilities and colors it. It's like putting a filter on their technique, putting a color on their technical strengths. They're not generic—they're individual and special. And anyone would make a grave mistake in saying that Laurent Tobel was not artistic. [His skating] is the most artistic thing I've ever seen. He has a kind of shocking, almost monstrous, strength behind him. But it's like comparing Charlie Chaplin to Sir Laurence Olivier—two different kinds of art. But equal at the end of the day.

Art has a great deal to do with emotion. I would like to think it's conscious, but maybe it's unconscious. I couldn't be precise about that. But I think it's thoughtful. I think that, say, Christopher Dean, with his approach to skating, is thoughtful. It isn't really by accident. It isn't just him doing his thing. Oleg Protopopov—I think that there really aren't too many minds in the world that know more about the art of skating than he does. [These two skaters] understand what they're doing. That intelligence and that understanding tend to become greater with age. I think I understand more now, certainly, about it than I did when I was 20.

Art and ego are joined at the hip. You gotta have that pat on the back. You gotta have the feedback. I know that I did. But [art] is also launched with emotion.

There really are only two crimes that can be committed, and if either one is, you're dead in the water. One is bad taste. You cannot achieve greatness launching yourself from vulgarity. The other is superficial emotions or phoniness, which we always have rammed down our throats with ice dancing.

You cannot be phony and you cannot be vulgar. If you can get over that, you can kind of launch yourself to greatness. If you're destined to be great.

JULIE MARCOTTE

Art through Passion

When a door closes, look around—there's probably a window open somewhere.

Six months after winning the Canadian Junior Dance Championship at the age of 17, Julie Marcotte's skating career was essentially over. During practice on a tour, another skater's blade sliced into her calf muscle. The wound necessitated 75 stitches to close, a long time in a cast to heal and a lot of thought about the future.

She got into coaching, and from there drifted into choreography when some young students required show programs. That was the thin edge of what was to become a very big wedge. In the next seven years she designed nearly 400 programs, and became one of the most sought-after choreographers in her country, despite having no training "except my dancing career and my passion for music."

When she was six or seven years old she used to gather all the children on her block together for special occasions such as birthdays and design a dance. "My mother pointed out to me the connection between what I am doing now and what I did when I was little," she says with a laugh.

Marcotte, who brings a definite French-Canadian flair to her programs, does most of her work by feel, sensing what will bring out the soul in her students and what will not.

I don't want to take anything away from the other provinces or the other mentality, even the States. But I find that in the French mentality we have a big, big European influence on us. I think [we're] a little warmer. Even in our attitudes. Not that the English people are cold . . . I don't know, it's just different. There is no limit. You can go and try anything and have fun with anything. We dare more with the artistic side than what English people are going to do. They're more, like with their personality, more into technical. Like you're going to talk to an Ontarian coach in dance and it's going to be so technical—"Look at this step," and "Look at that step." Which is excellent. But you have to be able to do both. These days the artistic side is going to be very important. Big, big, big, big-time. Often, it's going to take over more from the technical.

The bottom line of marks—that's me. What's artistic? In dance it's often going to be in the connection between two people. The way that they feel together and the way that they can feel a certain kind of music. And the way that they can express it on the ice. But it's all to themselves...you know what I mean? The way that they feel good doing it. And then you're going to get *them* to be artists, and get them to express it the way *they* feel it, how it's inside of them.

What I do is, I give them an initiation, I give them a drive. From there I let them take the road and drive to wherever they want. Sometimes along the road I'm going to help them, let's say, take that exit—to experience *that* a little more—and from there they're going to go to another road and they're going to keep driving. You have to use a different way of going to get it from inside of each person, but everybody has it. Deep down inside, no matter how stuck the person is.

I'm a very excited person. I get very emotional. I'd say 98 percent of the time, I'm very high...high on life. I have fun with not much. So often, when I have fun with the kids, they don't feel a barrier with me, so it's easier for them to be able to express themselves. So I take it from when we have fun, and I make them feel good about it. And then slowly and slowly, they're going to be able to let it all out and feel good about it.

In singles, it's the same thing again. The difference is that you don't have the connection with the other person. But you're going to have the connection with the judges. You're going to have the connection with the stands, and more connections within yourself, with your own feelings. You're going to go deeper into how you feel and express it from ri-i-i-ght in the stomach.

In dance and in pairs it's really the magic between two people. You're going to get to find something that you're never going to be able to find with someone else. Because it is so special, because skating is your passion and you share that passion with someone else. Whenever you can get it to connect between two people, the artistic speaks for itself. You don't even have to try. It just shines out of you.

My ears are always open. If I go see a movie. If I'm in a shopping center. Wherever I am, in the car, my ears are always open. At home I listen to music. But just to listen. I like everything. I love alternative rock. I love dance music. I love classical music. I l-o-o-o-o-ove jazz. I love blues. It always depends how I'm feeling.

I do music with another person, so I'll maybe call him and say, "I don't know, for this kid, I feel he could skate to this kind of music," and he's going to search on his side and I'm going to search on my side. But it often comes from the kids. When you go to a competition, you just look at them, and when a kind of music starts playing, you're going to see them move and be happy just listening to that kind of music. So, that's how I pick music, just by the way they feel the music.

I don't study them . . . I feel them.

ELVIS STOJKO

I Am Who I Am

In a perfect world, Elvis Stojko would never feel the need to speak up about his artistry. But skating is not a perfect world. It's not even close. Because of regular attacks on his artistic component, Stojko is constantly pushed to defend his choices of interpretation.

Although outsiders are content to dismiss Stojko as a brilliant athlete—and he is certainly that, as his quad–triple combination twice within two weeks in 1997 reconfirmed—the three-time World champion analyzes the process of presentation far more thoroughly than most elite skaters.

And process itself is part of art. Good stroking; powerful and confident delivery; knowing the difference between motion and movement; extending energy forces from one segment of the program through the next without interruption; sensing when to drive the music and when to let the music drive you—these are all as important to the art form as having been born with long, straight legs.

On tour in Los Angeles, Stojko was visited backstage by octogenarians Thayer Niklaus and Paula Kelly, legendary dancers in their time. "They wanted to tell me that they love what I'm doing and to continue," he recounts, beaming. "If someone says the style's not there, I can just sort of say to myself, 'Well, the cream of the crop is telling me it's there.' And that has given me a lot of momentum after taking a lot of bashing on that side."

Stojko—naturally a bit shy, and a deep believer in the stoic mental discipline of the martial arts—normally does not like to sell himself verbally. But he gets passionate and quite verbose about his on-ice creativity, especially if you broach the subject of his alleged artistic shortcomings.

I'm not into gimmicks. I'm into who I am. I've always had that confidence in me, knowing that what I'm doing is right for me, and I'm going to stick by it, no matter what anyone says. The crowd understands when you're being honest on the ice and when it's just pasted on.

All the choreography is mine. Everything since I've been working with Uschi [Keszler] is mine. But the whole idea is Uschi's. Working with me on getting the smile at the beginning, getting the line, working on the edge quality so you can gain momentum without having to scratch and make noise, and getting more of me out there. To be an artist, you have to have your own perception and you have to draw your own picture. If someone tells you you have to do this movement, this gesture, have this way of thinking, that's not really being an artist. Because someone's implanting those things in you.

Movement goes from point A to B. With motion, there is flow in between and it continues. And you can use them both. They always say a skater is doing movements. They do a pose—they do another pose—they do another pose. They're hitting all the poses, but there's no motion involved. There's no connection. You don't get a sense of flow as they're doing it, boom, boom, boom, boom, boom. Just little dynamic things click it up, make a difference. Actually change your way of thinking, your perception. You can skate to a piece of music one way and it doesn't look good. You do the same movement to a different piece of music, boom. It's all dynamics. It's in the context of the perception of the person watching.

I know who I am. I know I'm an artist on the ice. I know I'm a stylist in what I do. I'm happy, and I think that's a big thing for me. No one asked me before if I knew what I was doing. They'd just tell me I have to work on it.

Earlier, the judges hadn't connected with what I do. They were so into skating having to be "this way" that if they didn't see anything that resembled "this way," then it wouldn't be artistry. That's baloney. They have to open the realm of it and say, "Okay, what are the things involved—emotion, movement, motion, the care, that everything is connected."

There are different ways you can connect to the audience. A show program you can have fun with, you make eye contact with the audience. Then there are other times where you do specific movements on the ice not directed toward them, and people react to what you've just done. That's another connection to the audience, because it's aesthetically pleasing. There's a certain way you skate—an understanding of motion and movement and gliding—that creates that look, that gets people involved, spellbound. It's weird. People look back at the martial arts program of 1994. At the time they didn't like what I was doing, and now people say, "Wow, that was a classic artistic program." It was always there. It's just that people didn't see it because they didn't open their eyes to understand it. And I don't blame people for that, because things change, and if you're constantly looking at the one thing it's hard to open up.

A lot of male skaters will have very strong legs, and they don't use the upper body as much. I'm constantly using my upper body. A lot of people say, "You look like a gymnast. You look like a wrestler. You don't look like a figure skater." Okay, I may not look like a typical figure skater, but everyone has a different shape and size. Kulik is six foot, 145 pounds. I'm five foot seven, 155 pounds. If everybody looked [like Kulik], it'd be boring. You hear, "That's the classic, the perfect body type." I don't consider anybody the perfect body type, even myself. But certain movements might not look good on certain people because of body type.

It's not how long you are. It's if you hit the line. Within that you can create shapes.

I'm on that pathway of doing something different. I didn't choose to. I just ended up doing it that way because that's what feels right for me.

What I do on the ice as an artist is everything I've learned to this point. Everything I learned last year creates what I'm doing this year. So no one is going to skate the same. We're not born to go through the exact same things.

PHILIPPE CANDELORO

If They Don't Understand, It's Not Art

Philippe Candeloro is known for his single-theme choreography. When he was the surprise bronze medal winner at the 1994 Olympics, he skated both his short and long programs to music from the same movie, The Godfather. *All his programs tend to be constructed around easily identifiable characters. Some observers, such as Toller Cranston and Alexei Mishin, Alexei Urmanov's coach, consider it vulgar. Others find it refreshing and a necessary alternative.*

Early in his career Candeloro, like so many of the world's elite men skaters, treated choreography like high-school Latin homework: to be endured but not embraced. "I was very interested in the jumps and the speed, but not in artistic

impression and putting one hand up in the air. I was afraid that my friends on
the hockey team would laugh at me."

Now if anyone laughs at his performance, it's because that's what he intended.

For me, the art is not something special. It's not only one thing. Art is many things. An artist gives something new and gives pleasure because the people who watch the art receive and understand something. If people can see an art and not understand what it is, it is not art—this is what I think. Art is making people understand, and it has to be new. And maybe one person can give a lot of different art to a lot of different people. This is what I want to do.

If I were a painter I'd do relief pictures. I don't like to copy a style. I don't like to listen to only one music. I can listen to all kinds of music—classic, pop, rap, rock, jazz—but not for a long time. I cannot listen to one CD for 60 minutes.

For two years after Lillehammer, I think the people and the judges and the ISU understood the new style of skating. They supported Elvis and me on the new style of skating. Now I have the impression that they came back to where they were. They progressed and then they came back. I don't know why. But this is what I feel. They prefer the style of the Russians, Urmanov and Kulik, and Eldredge. It's more classical. It's more like American skating. It's not like theater.

If we can get a lot of people watching skating on TV it's because there are some skaters like Stojko and me on the ice to give them a new concept of skating. Because people like stronger men. Now the people think figure skating is very good to watch. It's manly.

Urmanov's coach said in the paper I was ugly on the ice. And that is everyone's view, because they read the paper. I didn't have any feelings about that. Maybe the newspaper people changed the article or something like that. But my coach talked with Urmanov's coach and he said, "That's true. What they said in the paper, that's true. This is what I think. Everyone has the right to think." All right. But every skater has the right to skate the way he wants. We need some of the Urmanov types, too, to make it different from the Stojko and Candeloro types.

KURT BROWNING

That Overall Glow

Kurt Browning is The Natural. He confesses that he is also The Ham. He loves to perform and be recognized for it. Appreciation is, after all, the currency of artistry.

Although he originally gained fame for his athleticism—he's in the record books for doing the first quadruple jump—Browning has evolved into one of the great skating entertainers of our time, closing the gap between himself and Scott Hamilton as King of the Showmen.

Besides his energy, speed, irrepressible sense of humor and unerring ability to gauge his audience, Browning brings an extraordinary versatility to the sport. There are few styles that he has not attempted and mastered. While he was the consummate amateur competitor, winning four World titles, he is better suited to the professional arena, where there are no rules of decorum, no preconceived musical notions, and where disbelief is willingly suspended.

Veteran choreographer Sandra Bezic—who designed the famous Casablanca *adieu to his amateur career—could not believe that Browning had not received formal dance training, he so readily understands the relationship between music and movement.*

When he is not touring with Stars on Ice, competing on the pro circuit or making TV specials, Browning is with his wife, Sonja Rodriguez, a dancer with the National Ballet of Canada.

I'm a parrot, a total mime. I watch and learn and listen. I get inspired watching Torvill and Dean and watching Sonja. I think I've been influenced by the ballet, watching Sonja and the way the guys dance. I see what they do in ballet and see how uninhibited they are. You just can't move that way unless you're uninhibited.

I did this one piece that was all East Indian folklore, I mean, how strange is that? But I didn't realize that it was being strange. I had this choreographer, Brian Power, and he'd always been influenced by the way [East Indians] move and he just sold me on it. He'd say, "When you take your hands like this and flip them over, that means it's a waterfall and it's the ever-flowing of life." I didn't even think that it might not be cool or that it might be weird. I just liked the music, I had fun with it and I went with it. Call it "ignorance is bliss."

When I did *Casablanca*, that was me looking at the movie going, "Oh, that's so cool. Humphrey Bogart is absolutely smooth, suave, cool." And who wouldn't want to try to be like that? It just seemed so much easier to compete when I had something else to think about, when the character was as important as the triple Axel and when the two were tied together. Humphrey Bogart would not miss the triple Axel. He wouldn't.

Halfway through a number, if I'm not getting any help from an audience, it's really hard. I usually go more for them, or I kind of give up on them.

I'll get better as the number goes on if the audience is liking it, because my confidence just soars. I suppose it's like that in competition. There was a moment in Ottawa when I was pretty sure I had the Toyota Canadian Pro won and it came time for the triple loop and I'm thinking, "I've got this thing won. I don't need this triple loop." And I look up in the audience and everyone is smiling and I go, "Oh, God, we're all having a good time. There's no way I'm going to miss this triple loop. Hey, they want one. Yeah, let's go!" It was totally the audience that urged me on. I think that a good showman allows the audience to persuade or change or move him.

I think I've always been a showman. I've always enjoyed having everyone in the room stare at me. I've never been shy or anything.

I'm always surprised that you feel the same way in the tunnel going out to the ice. Maybe you're really depressed, or maybe you've just had bad news from home or you've been injured. It doesn't matter what the situation is. When it comes your turn to entertain you just want it so badly. Because the difference between stepping off the ice having skated well and [stepping off the ice] having skated badly is like the difference between someone kissing you or someone punching you in the gut. Total opposite.

You just want that overall glow you get from performing well. You want it every single time. It's like a drug.

SHAE-LYNN BOURNE

The Most Political of All

You could make an argument that Shae-Lynn Bourne and Victor Kraatz might have been outpoliticked for the silver medal at the 1997 World Championships. They had defeated defending silver medalists Anjelika Krylova and Oleg Ovsiannikov handily at the Grand Prix Final two weeks before, with a 5–2 split in judges. Both couples stepped up their level of skating at Worlds, but it was a different judging panel and a 6–3 split for the Russians in the free dance. In fact, Krylova and Ovsiannikov were nearly as close to winners Oksana Grischuk and Evgeny Platov (they had two first places) as they were to the Canadians.

In the corridors of the arena at Worlds, there was a lot of huddling among national federation representatives, and much of the talk was about dance. Favors may have been traded off; they may not have been. But the Canadians know that for the Olympics, their representatives have to be part of those huddles.

I think the dance discipline is probably the most political of them all. The whole sport is very political, and I knew that when I got into it. I didn't know the depth of it until I got into the dance world, though.

In fact, it wasn't until 1996 that I saw how political it was. I think before that we were both very naive and blind. We just skated.

Last year, I think our eyes opened from all the years we'd already been through. Dance is not like pairs or singles, where you can just move up from the compulsories to the original dances—two or three spots. There are a lot of times when people have really bad compulsories and an amazing original, but that can't happen in ice dancing judging. It's a full-package deal. When you're out there practicing, that's when you're being judged. You have to be good in the compulsory, OD and free. Equally.

Is it fair? Actually, I don't think so. If you're good in the compulsories, sure, be up there. But if your OD's not good, then be judged that way.

Victor and I are in the sport at the right time. Right now, the Russians are still leading, but we're in the medals. The whole sport is changing. It has accepted the North American style and that hasn't happened in a long time. I think people can feel that there could be a change.

I get a kick out of competing in dance. Ever since I started, I've just been very relaxed in the dance event. I don't know how the men are, but as far as the women go, when you get in the dressing room it can be very catsy. And that's not just in the dance. It's in the women's event, too. Catsy, and they play games.

But for me, I feel like an outsider because I just smile. I have such a great time and nothing affects me. I can see what's going on and I just laugh.

NATALIA DUBOVA

From Russia, with Politics

Before the Iron Curtain was raised, the three leading dance coaches in the world were all living in Russia: Natalia Dubova, Natalia Linichuk and Tatiana Tarasova.

The trio still coaches the top three dance couples in the world, but now all three are living in the United States. Tarasova is in Boston, where she handles 1994 Olympic winners Oskana Grischuk and Evgeny Platov. Linichuk, who used to have Grischuk and Platov, is in Newark, Delaware, with Anjelika Krylova and Oleg Ovsiannikov. And Dubova, who also used to coach Grischuk and Platov, is in Lake Placid with Canadians Shae-Lynn Bourne and Victor Kraatz.

It is no secret that there is no love lost, professionally speaking, among the three Russian coaches. Nor that there are constant political battles raging behind the scenes as the coaches and their support staff lobby for judging favor in a discipline where judging preference plays a much bigger role than in singles or pairs.

Dubova worked at the Spartak Club in Moscow for 36 years, but when the economic and social structure of the then Soviet Union began to change quickly and unpredictably, she decided to leave. That decision was hastened when her husband had emergency heart bypass surgery in San Francisco during the 1989 Tom Collins tour. "People in the U.S. really helped me because I felt very alone," she recalls. "I feel I can return my thank-you if I give this country all my professional energy."

While Dubova says she does not like all the politics in ice dancing, she can do a little politicking of her own, as you'll see in the following discussion.

Politics? In dancing we don't have any jumps or spins, not so many elements, and coaches and judges can use that because the problem is you like it or you don't like it. My personal feeling is that when I worked with the Russian athletes they were really the best on the market. Russia did traditionally the best ice dancing. But I don't think it's fair if they are dominant just for tradition, if the athletes don't show the quality of skating.

Let's see what we see today. The ISU Technical Committee talks about the ice dancing must be merely dancing—close to ballroom dance, dance music, lots of positions, lots of things going on, really dancing. Why we follow this rule and other ones don't do it and try to win? They don't show any dancing, any difficult moves. They dance tragic on ice. Some skate like with the pain, and when the audiences don't understand it, probably they think, "What they don't understand? It's so great!" I think what crowd likes is what crowd understands. This is best because we do it for people.

I just keep going to show ice dancing world that the couple with whom I work today improved each day, each practice, each competition. And I tell my students, in ice dancing you need to be like two steps ahead to win.

I'm not really big fan where it must be like ballroom dance. But if Technical Committee already decided it, probably we must follow. Or if you do not agree, we must change the rules. But if the rule's there, we need to follow it to have everybody compete fair. I don't know what other coaches are thinking, but Bourne and Kraatz did the continental tango [in their 1997 original dance], which is a close position with a lot of dancing. Which I didn't see from Krylova and Ovsiannikov. It was very sharp what Russians did, but if you were to take off music, you can tell they could do it to different music.

I actually don't pay a lot of attention how somebody lives. I'm thinking the country where you move, U.S. or Canada, easily can live without us. That's why when you come, you need to forget who you were and start everything from the beginning and show the world you did it for Russia because you can do it, and start doing it for the country for which you're going to work. We live in the States and do a good business with Canada because we live close to Canada. I don't do anything against Russia. I do my best for my new country.

I am very proud that country trusts me and gives me a chance to work with the most talented students with whom I work in my life. I think they are more talented than Klimova and more than Usova and more than Grischuk, and I tell you why. Because right now ice dancing is more athletic, and also ice dancing need to be more natural emotion. And Shae and Vic have lots of potential because they're great technically, great positive people. They're athletes. Great open vision to learn. And they concentrate.

Sometimes I can compare because I know the other mentality, mentality of Russia. Sometimes [Russian skaters] are only motivated until they feel they already can make money or something like that. Also here, if you find the people who concentrate, it works much better. Here kids have a lot of choice in their life. In Russia, in my time, only probably sport opened the door to the West countries.

I think Russian dancers can be beaten, and it will be very soon if they don't start making new skaters with very good basic skating and technique. Bourne and Kraatz, already you don't speak about technique. It is much, much higher because they can do anything. It is a pleasure to watch them. And if you come to performance you want to have a pleasure.

OTTAVIO CINQUANTA

Why I am Very Good to Judges

Since ascending to the presidency of the International Skating Union, Ottavio Cinquanta has aggressively promoted the ISU's proprietary interest in the sport.

To broaden its base of interest, he wants skating to be simpler for mass audiences to understand: which could be dreaming the impossible dream.

While he actively protects ISU judges, he has publicly pushed for several changes to the scoring process. Concerned about confusing results at the 1997 Europeans, he began seeking adjustments to the "majority placement" system. He was concerned that a skater who does not have a chance to win but draws last to skate in the long program can change the standings of the top three. He was also investigating providing judges with television instant replays for the short program.

Cinquanta has a colorful manner, even in his second language, of describing situations. An example is his mock conversation with Dick Button.

Why am I very good to the judges? Why? Why? Because the difference between us and the others is our judges. Bad or good. Sufficient or insufficient. Proactive or old-fashioned.

I say to my friend Dick Button, between us and you, there are our judges.

Between a show and a competition, what is the difference? The presence of the judges.

"Oh, but your judges are no good."

"Who says so?"

"Everybody."

"Come on, everybody who? Yamaguchi, maybe? Boitano, maybe? Petrenko? All these people? When they were awarded the gold medal of the Olympic Games, the ISU judges were okay, permitting them to earn a million dollars. Now these judges are no good? This is inconsistent."

I have the duty to try to improve the judging situation, and you know that I'm trying very hard to do that. I am brave enough to try to break this situation in the ISU, but provided everybody respects our judges. Because I am not available to be in trouble through the criticism of our judges who are working for nothing, who are not paid, who are dedicating all their free time and more than their free time.

Exactly the difference that exists between the sport of the podium and the sport of the entertainment and the dollars is the judges. That is what I want to protect.

BRUCE HYLAND

Friend of Figures

Bruce and Marg Hyland own Center Ice, a popular rink in Countryside Mall in Clearwater, Florida. At Center Ice they teach programs from both the United States Figure Skating Association and an alternative organization, Ice Skating International. ISI was invented by Michael Kirby and brought into the Ice Capades system. It offers its own World Championships, and there is a graduated system of competition levels, based on achieving certain technical standards. Hyland likes it because it has the same discipline in free skating that used to be encouraged by compulsory figures.

Before leaving in 1977 to manage an Ice Capades Chalet in California, Hyland ran skating schools in Canada, and was renowned for coaching the Jelineks to the World pairs title in 1962 and Debbie Wilkes and Guy Revell to an Olympic silver medal.

Many North American coaches, Hyland among them, bemoan the fact that beginning in 1991, figures were no longer contested in the major championships of the sport that had "figure" right in its name.

That meant that elite skaters no longer practiced figures, and very few skaters at the lower levels now come into contact with what was once considered the very heart of the game.

They should never have gotten rid of them. It was training and discipline that skating was all about when it first started. It's the discipline of being able to maintain a proper edge and proper balance. [The absence of figures is] now showing up in the next generation. These children are coming in and dealing with moves in the field, and they want rockers and counters and brackets and they don't have any training. They don't even know what a rocker is. It's very difficult because the kids are trying to do these fast moves, so you have to start teaching them a rocker and a counter on a circle, just as if they're doing figures anyway. That wouldn't have been a problem if they had their basic figures.

When figures were in their prime, skaters would do at least two or three hours a day, then two or three hours of freestyle. All my pairs skaters, even, did figures because of the discipline. Without them, it's like a musician not doing any scales. It's the same thing.

Anyone at the World Championship level today has still gone through figures. It's 10 years from now that you'll see the effect. I can see more skaters like Surya Bonaly—no edges and very acrobatic. You need control and the edges when you come down.

It isn't hard to jump out of a ten-story building, but it's hard to land.

JOHN NICKS

Seven Counterarguments

John Nicks coached American skaters to 37 gold medals in compulsory figures. So one would assume that he would be among those sad to see them go.

Assume again. While Nicks liked "school figures, in a way, for school figures' sake," he does not agree that they were the foundation for good free skating. Quite the contrary, actually.

He says the best example is in the professional shows, where young skaters who haven't had contact with figures because they haven't come through the competitive system are "wonderful free skaters."

He offers seven arguments against the figures–freestyle theory of relativity.

Having expertise in school figures had nothing to do with freestyle ability. In freestyle, for instance, speed over the ice is very important. It's exciting. In school figures, speed over the ice is something that's not required, and even coached against. In good school figures, skaters take off at the slowest possible speed and try with continuous flow to get around a paragraph figure. So excitement and speed, which are good for freestyle, are really not required for school figures at all.

In freestyle, an important thing is audience reaction to a skater. That reaction is often associated with the skater looking at the audience, playing to the audience. In freestyle we very rarely coach any skater to look down at the ice for any length of time. In school figures, it's just the opposite. You certainly don't go around looking up at an audience—you pay attention to the ice.

A good freestyle skater has emotion and artistry. Emotion really is very bad in school figures. The finest figures skaters are basically machines—they repeat the same thing three or six times, depending upon the requirements. In freestyle, with the difference in tempo, emotions have to change.

In freestyle, there has to be great physical courage. Often, there's a lot of hurt and injury associated with it. Often, when you teach advanced jumping, you're going to ask a skater who's fallen on a hip perhaps four or five times to do it again. That sort of courage, that physical courage, is not needed in school figures. People very rarely fall down and hurt themselves. I'm not saying there shouldn't be mental courage in figures. There should be. But it's not the same sort of courage at all.

The great freestylist has to have a wonderful appreciation and knowledge of music. Of course appreciation and knowledge of music are not needed for the school figures at all. The only time I ever heard music is when I used to go out and teach patch early in the morning and some of the kids used to play music while they were doing figures. When I asked them why they did that, they said it was to take their mind off the figures. I let them play it because it took my mind off having to *teach* the figures.

The psychological makeup of a wonderful school figure skater I found to be totally different from a wonderful freestylist. And with all due respect, the figure skaters who have done beautiful figures have usually not been particularly strong in freestyle. And unfortunately the great freestylers who did well in figures only usually did well in figures because they were great freestylers.

The only reason I've heard that school figures contribute anything is in control of edges and turns. But I don't agree there, because if you're talking about turns in school figures, it's very important that you have a clean edge going in and a clean edge going out of a turn. Certainly the turn is not jumped at all. You're taught to press on the ice to make sure that that edge is in and the edge is out. The greatest footwork skaters around now—Browning, Wylie, Hamilton—you put a camera on their feet when they're doing footwork and they don't touch the ice on turns. So what you're teaching in school figures for a perfect turn is exactly opposite from what you'd teach for footwork in freestyle.

And really I could go on and on and on. I'm absolutely convinced.

VICTOR KRAATZ

A Bird That Cannot Fly

No North American ice dancers have ever won a World or Olympic championship, but a Canadian couple training in the U.S. may become the first.

The rise of Shae-Lynn Bourne and Victor Kraatz at the world level was rapid, especially for non-Russians: 14th in 1993, to 6th, to 4th, to bronze medals in 1996 and 1997. They, and many others, feel they're as good as or better than the two Russian couples ranked ahead of them.

Bourne and Kraatz joined forces in a "well, it can't hurt to try" audition in April of 1991, and from the first few turns around the ice, it was automatic chemistry, despite their different backgrounds. Bourne is from small-town Ontario and Kraatz has lived in three, now four, countries. He was born in Germany and raised in Switzerland—he was national junior dance champion—before moving to Canada in 1987.

His parents always encouraged him to play sports, but he didn't get into skating until the relatively late age of 10, because, like everyone else in his alpine town, he was out on the slopes.

Because Kraatz was a skier and Bourne was a pairs skater, they bring a hearty athleticism to ice dancing. Their soft knees and their originality often have them compared to Torvill and Dean.

They're best known for inventing the technique of hydroblading, an angular low-to-the-ice technique that requires tremendous knowledge and control of fulcrums and forces.

Shae-Lynn and I, and Uschi Keszler and a variety of other skaters, Elvis among them, had this great thing going where a whole bunch of us got together when we trained in Philadelphia and Montreal and threw ideas at one another. It got to a point where no new ideas came in, and it started getting stale. So Shae-Lynn and I started playing with things.

Initially, we started hydroblading just leaning on pylons for support. Then I said, "If we do it with pylons, why not do it with Rollerblading wrist guards, to get lower, to get a better angle out of it?"

We had these ideas, and one year later we had a whole number that was just hydroblading. We skated it on the Tom Collins Tour in 1993, to Pink Floyd. We showed what skating was before, then showed the modern type, which was close to the ground.

People say that they do hydroblading, but it's not the moves that make it. It's more the understanding of how the energy acts on the body. Where you have your weight on the blade while you do certain moves will determine which direction you go in—straight, left or right. Plus, whether you're supporting your partner, or vice versa. People try to copy these moves and say, "I'm hydroblading," but they're just copycats. They don't put the time and effort in to really understand the technique.

I'm not complaining about it. I just wish people would take the time to experiment with it themselves, add something to it, so skating will grow.

Hydroblading took off in one practice at the Lillehammer Olympics. I don't believe in horoscopes, but it's like how they say the stars are aligned. We had the right moment at the right time in the right place when we decided to practice hydroblading at the Olympics.

The German and Norwegian television picked it up and we did interviews the next day. It was our first Olympics, and we placed 10th, and it just took off from there. And it all came from that one moment in practice. All of a sudden people were saying, "They are a couple to watch!"

Very deep inside I'm this skater who just likes to train. And that's what I'm best at. I like to train and then I like to perform what I train. That's why, at the

World Championship, I don't get nervous per se anymore, because I know I did everything I could.

Good skating is the way you skate on your edges and the understanding of what the blade can do. Unlike Elvis, who leaves the ice, I'm what I call a kiwi, a bird that cannot fly, that just sort of runs. I've never had the feeling of leaving the ice and jumping. I'm sort of grounded to the ice. I've got that perfect connection with the ice. And I'm lucky. The way I'm built, I'm suited for this one skill, ice dancing. I learned that from the beginning. In Switzerland all I wanted to do is learn the skills—forward, backward, standing on your feet, shoot the duck, all those kinds of things. I started doing tests, and it was always challenging for me because skating is a totally different sport from skiing.

The misconceptions arise when people say, "You should have a little more fun." "You should go out and party." I look at it a little differently right now, because I like to train and I like to feel well. I sometimes see athletes go to a party and the next day they train and they don't feel the greatest. I don't like that feeling. It's the same when I'm tired. If you look at the body as being a machine, I like when your engine runs on all cylinders. My dream is to be the best, and not mediocre.

I don't have too many friends, but the friends I have, I can see them get sidetracked into doing other things. Maybe that works for them, but I know it wouldn't work for me.

By the time I stop skating—and you never know when that will come, it could be through injury or whatever—I want to know that until that moment I did the best I could. I never want to say afterward, "Maybe I should have treated the situation differently."

I'm lucky enough to know Simone, Natalia Dubova's husband. He used to be an athlete. He wanted to succeed, as well, really badly. But because at the time he was competing for the Soviet Union, the government decided who was going to go to the Olympics, who was going to go to the Worlds, and he, I believe, never got to fulfill his dream. I don't want to have that same feeling. I want to fulfill my dream and go out of the sport with a good feeling.

And then leave it behind.

LUCINDA RUH

As Swiss as Chocolate

There are minor hints that the art of spinning is making a comeback, but for Swiss skaters it never left.

Switzerland has been blessed with an uninterrupted lineage of brilliant spinners for more than a quarter century. The most renowned, of course, was 1981 World champion Denise Biellmann, after whom the distinctive and seemingly impossible toe-above-the-head spin is named. But Biellmann took the baton from countrywoman Karin Iten, another superior twirler.

In recent years, two other Swiss women have made audiences dizzy watching their rapid revolutions. Natalie Krieg once spun continuously for three minutes and 22 seconds, and Lucinda Ruh is the most visually effective spinner among today's amateurs.

One theory is that the Swiss had cramped rinks that offered little space to do the big tricks, so they spent more time on spinning. But that would not explain the prowess of Ruh, who many say out-Biellmanns Biellmann with her back-arching revolutions. Ruh lived in Switzerland for only the first eight months of her life, then moved to Paris, then to Japan at the age of four, where she grew up. She now trains in California with Christy Ness, after studying under Toller Cranston.

Ruh was a serious ballet student, and was offered a scholarship to London's Royal Ballet School when she was eight. After a summer in England assessing the program, she decided, instead, to stick with figure skating and returned home to Japan, where she was coached by Yuka Sato's father, Nabuo. "I like to be alone on the ice in front of big audiences," she says.

Although Ruh finished 19th, 18th and 15th in her first three World Championships, she is in demand as a show skater because of those spins.

And forget about asking her to let you in on the trade secrets: she doesn't know them.

We were living in Japan. My dad traveled back to Switzerland for work and came back and told me he saw Biellmann do the Biellmann spin.

He really thought that I should keep up the tradition and do it, too. He worked hard with me off and on the ice to do that spin. We tried everything possible to make my back more flexible.

Just before Christmas, when I was nine, I said to him, "Come to the rink." His Christmas present was...I could do the spin. He was, like, so happy.

I've never talked to Denise Biellmann, but I've seen her skate, and I think it's amazing that she can keep it up. I just don't know what it is about Switzerland and spinning. Even our little novice boy is a great spinner. Maybe ballet did help my skating. It could have—I don't really know. I didn't really do anything to help my spins. I just practiced them.

People keep asking me what it takes to spin like that. And I really don't know. It feels really nice. It feels just like I could spin forever in that position. It's like people who can really jump well. I guess it's just the feeling. On Elvis's TV show, he said to me, "Can you teach me to spin?" and I said, "Only if you can teach me to do the quad." In San Francisco just for fun, I tried once with some pupils of Mrs. Ness to teach them spinning. It's really difficult, because when I spin, I'm not thinking of what I'm doing. When I jump, I'm really thinking about what I have to do, but the spin is more natural. So it's hard to teach someone what I was doing because I don't know what I was doing.

When a spin isn't going well, it feels kind of wobbly. But most of the time I can recenter it, even if it's going off a little. Like Elvis. If he goes up on a jump on an angle, he can still land it. I never really get dizzy. I think that's mostly practice. In the beginning I got dizzy, but not after that. I don't pick a spot to focus on. Sometimes I close my eyes.

It just feels like you're in another place, not on the ice. It's hard to describe. It's like you're in your own world.

MANDY WÖTZEL

Ouch!

Popular German pairs skaters Mandy Wötzel and Ingo Steuer were able to win their first World Championship in 1997 because they skated well—and because they were able to stay out of ambulances.

They are probably the most dramatic injury-prone twosome in skating. At the

1994 Olympic Games, Wötzel had to be carried off the ice when she smashed her jaw during a routine moment in their long program. The pair was forced to withdraw from the Games.

And at a practice during Skate Canada 1993, Wötzel knocked Steuer out as she was coming down from a lift. At a pro-am in late 1996, she loosened one of his front teeth with an errant elbow.

Even with her previous partner, Axel Rauschenbach, there was the dark cloud of injury. After a horrifying training accident, Wötzel fell into a coma and the pair had to skip the 1989 Worlds at Paris.

She is forced to concede that there are safer ways to spend your time than getting thrown all over a rink.

Yes, pairs skating is dangerous. You're with a partner, and it's not only that you can fall from a jump on the ice, you can also fall from a lift because your partner takes the wrong step or something like that.

I've gotten used to it now. I was so young when I started that it was something new. I cannot explain the feeling. The lift is maybe like [being] a bird. But the throws you have to land alone. It's something different. At first it seemed like a long way, but I'm used to it now. I like being thrown sometimes, but if there is something different between us, then I'm afraid. Sometimes you feel slower than usual, and so you are not straight in the air. It doesn't matter for the landing, but in the air you don't feel so good. Sometimes you have the wrong feeling.

I'm not scared that often. But if the day or the whole week is stressful, and you have to hurry up with your practice, and you have a lot of work after the practice, then you are into a stress situation. And then it can happen that you are afraid to jump or be thrown, and you have a wrong feeling.

There is no limit to what can happen. I can remember the Lillehammer fall. There were no steps. Just nothing. I fell. It was going into a spiral. And I fell and hurt my chin. I cannot believe this. It's the Olympic Games. It can happen in practice. Small children in practice can get hurt. You can fall and hit your chin crossing the street. Everybody has fallen on the chin sometime or other. But the Olympics? You are nervous before the competition, and when I fell I went into shock. And when I got the stitches, the doctor said, "Better you don't skate."

At Skate Canada, Ingo got hurt on a twist lift. I didn't feel it—I'm just alone in the air. I tried to hold my arms really tight. But then Ingo caught me, and then he fell, and I placed my elbow in his teeth. It seemed like a half hour that he was lying on the ice blacked out. It was probably one minute or less, but it was a very long time for me, because I was thinking he was dead. He falls, and then he is lying there the whole time. I slugged him like in a boxer—what do you call it . . . a glass chin? We had to quit the competition. He had a black eye.

When I was skating with Axel Rauschenbach, sometimes he would fall on the lift, and that was not too good for the partner. When I was 15, I got blacked out twice. One time I fell from the lift and one time we did a camel spin too close together. I had his blade in my head. I cannot remember, because I blacked out right away. I have no idea how long I was out—nobody told me.

Why do I still [skate]? Because I love it. It's my sport. It's dangerous, but you could have a fight at school. You could go in the street and get hit. I mean, something can happen to you everywhere.

You do the elements so often during the season. If it happens one time, well, okay. If it happens to you daily, maybe it's better you stop.

KRIS WIRTZ

Nationals Calamity

There is just something about the Canadian Championships that seems to point Kris Wirtz toward the emergency ward. For three straight years, he had some calamity or another befall him during Nationals. In 1995, it was the near inability to breathe. The next year there was his spectacular fall and ensuing concussion during training for the free-skate final, which put him in the hospital overnight and left his and pairs partner Kristy Sargeant's participation in doubt. But he rallied, and the couple made the World team. In 1997, early in the free skate he was slammed just below the eye by Sargeant's elbow, bringing the pair an anxious sense of déjà vu. They again gutted their way through the performance, made the World team and moved up to a strong sixth place at Worlds.

When Wirtz burst out of the remote Ontario town of Marathon and onto the national scene in the late 1980s, he was a little rough around the edges. A little too wisecracking, a little too outspoken and a little too honest for skating to embrace immediately. But he has turned out to be one of the most responsible athletes on the Canadian team. He was team captain in 1997, and lives with his partner, helping raise her daughter, Triston.

He and Sargeant have finished second at nationals three times, and figure they will win one, if only Wirtz can stay healthy for the whole week.

It all started to landslide in about 1995. I had pneumonia—I had bronchitis—everything. I was stuffed up, couldn't breathe. When I get close to competition, my sleep hours shorten, I have trouble staying on the same schedule and get fatigued. In the excitement of getting ready for the competition, my immune system sort of slows down, and I didn't stay on the vitamins. So that was basically my fault, but it was pretty severe. I was puking like crazy. I don't even know how I did the program. Basically, when I looked at Kristy, I thought I was dead. We finished fifth, after going to the Olympics the year before.

In 1996, everything was going well. We'd had a great season heading into nationals at Ottawa. Then the practice for the long program. I could say I hit a rut—I could say anything. I didn't check, because I was out cold. What I remember was that when I popped back up and came to, everybody said, "Don't move, blah, blah, blah," and I was, like, "What's everybody's problem?"

The question was, "Kris, do you know where you are?" "Yes, I'm in Edmonton." I had reverted to Edmonton, January 1994. It was really February 1996. They asked me how old I was, and I said the age I was in 1994. So that was kind of weird. It was a scary moment.

I came off the ice under my own steam and I was going to get up and skate. Paul [Wirtz, his brother and coach] was getting aggressive with me because sometimes I tend to back off, and he said, "Now, get out there and do your footwork." I looked at Kristy and was saying, "Which footwork?" and I was again going back to the two-year-old program. I had no idea what I was doing…I was freaking out. I was like that boxer [Oliver McCall]. I almost had a nervous breakdown. Came off the ice, talked to the doctor, and that's when we all figured out that Kris was a little messed up in the melon.

At the hospital, the doctors were saying they were going to have to alleviate the pressure and they're going to have to drill. "Oh, you won't be able to skate because we're going to have to put you under." I was, like, "Holy crap, man." I was a little nervous.

But they didn't drill and I was able to skate the long program the next day. Knowing that if I fell and hit my head, it could cause severe, severe brain damage, I was a little nervous. I think it rubbed off on the team, because we didn't have a stellar performance.

Then the fire alarm went off halfway through the program and that was another situation. It seems that when one thing happens, it just snowballs. We were at the three-minute mark when it went off. I'd missed an element about three elements before—I did a "waxle." We could have begun over, but when it starts, that's the competition and that's it. I'm not a poor sport. If there's anything people can look back on in my skating career, it's that I'm a good sport.

So then, in 1997, when the week was going smoothly, I was, like, "No problem, Kris and Kristy are going to get their national championship." Because we've always said that if everything goes smooth we're going to win. Then we opened up the long program by once again—I don't know, I'm not going to even try and figure out why—getting hurt. Twenty seconds in, I got belted and almost knocked out. I was kind of woozy for about 45 seconds. I knew it was an elbow—you're a pairs guy you know that's what hits you. When it happened, I went, "Oh, my God, that hit me right in my eye. That baby's going to swell." After we did the throw triple Salchow, I kind of got my wits back. But I was sort of fazed. I was way out there. I was in lunar space. I was gone. It wasn't a performance to remember, but we learned from it and we know that we can overcome a lot of things.

I think what has a lot to do with it is that I'm not the biggest guy, for a pairs skater. So to deal with performing up to the level of all the other athletes in the pairs event, I have to go a little bit off the wall and be a little psychotic. So when I go, I go. I give it a shot. I go guns-out all the way. If I had another couple of inches, another ten pounds. . . . But that's that "if" factor. A lot of people could say if, if, if. I have what I have, and I accept what I've accomplished in my career. And I won't trade it for anything, because it's all Kris and Kristy's accomplishments.

PAUL COFFEY AND
STEVE YZERMAN

Figure Skating Was for Nerds

Power skating was invented by figure skaters working at the Tam O'Shanter
Summer Hockey School near Toronto in the early 1960s. It has been fine-tuned
over the decades, but it is still the same basic concept: applying figure skating's
understanding of blade and muscle use to hockey skating. Power skating is now
an integral part of hockey development programs throughout the United States
and Canada.

Paul Coffey and Steve Yzerman were teammates, briefly, for the Detroit Red
Wings of the National Hockey League. But while Yzerman has been a Red Wing
his entire career, Coffey moved on, and is now with the Philadelphia Flyers, the
fifth team of his career.

Both are headed for the Hall of Fame, both are known as excellent skaters and
both were growing up just as power skating began taking root as a way for players
to enhance their chances of moving up the hockey ladder.

They spoke about power skating during the 1997 NHL All-Star weekend in
San Jose, where, the previous winter, hometown hero Rudy Galindo had turned
in one of the most memorable performances in skating history.

Steve Yzerman

It was just starting when I was a kid. It was in its early stages. But I never took it.

However, I'll use Sheldon Kennedy as an example. His sister was a figure
skater and he told me that he was in figure skating for a couple of years when
he was a kid. And he's one of the best skaters I've ever seen. So obviously it
helped him.

Just getting power in your legs and developing your skating legs helps. I think
everyone has his own unique skating style, but you've got to be able to use a
stride and develop that power in your legs, and agility and things like

Power skating was around, but we just played. We went to hoc
the summers and played. Power skating was power skating.

Paul Coffey

I took it. It was Weston Power Skating School. It wasn't figure skating. It was all done by hockey people. It definitely wasn't figure skating. I wouldn't have gone if it was figure skating.

I went three or four summers in a row, probably from the age of 10 to 14. All my buddies were going to hockey school where you went away, and you skated an hour and you water-skied and you did all of that kind of stuff. I was never allowed to do that. My dad asked me if I wanted to go power skating, and I said sure.

I can't remember if I was a good and natural skater before that. I'm sure I had a gift, but I mean that kind of stuff hones your stride.

I just remember getting smacked on the ass. It wasn't like they taught you anything. It was just, like, you skated for an hour. You went in and out of pylons. You went under chairs. You did all that kind of stuff. You never touched a puck...you just skated.

Figure skaters—figure skating was for nerds. I never did that. I just did all those down-and-backs, one knee, two knees, up, back, just hustling, working.

Did they teach about edges? Not really. I think some of that stuff is overblown. I'm sure you can teach it, but a lot of stuff you don't want to jam it down guys' throats. Just go out and develop your own stride.

The Storytellers

PHILIP HERSH
Katarina Witt

Phil Hersh, who writes Olympic sports for the Chicago Tribune, *has been cover-ing figure skating on a regular basis since the Lake Placid Winter Games of 1980. Fluent in several languages, and a four-time nominee for the Pulitzer Prize, he is one of the major—if not the major—journalistic voices in American skating. As the cadre of American writers traveling to big-time competitions reconstitutes itself from era to era—journalists gain and lose interest, matching the career paths of hometown skaters or the ebb and flow of major stories—Hersh remains one of the few constants. He is a walking reference book for, and influ-ence upon, U.S. writers who have been parachuted into competition coverage or who lack his confidence with the complicated process of assessing a performance. He is opinionated and direct, often to the point of bluntness. One of his favorite sports is the good-natured verbal thrust and parry with Canadian writers, con-ducted at high-decibel levels.*

Above all, Hersh has an unerring eye for the story, and the story in the 1980s was, more often than not, Katarina Witt.

I could see the transformation of a whole political system through Katarina Witt. My first exposure to her was at the Sarajevo Olympics, only my sec-ond Olympics covering figure skating. What I remembered most about Sarajevo, which said so much about East Germany at that stage, was that in her post-championship press conference she answered questions fluently in English for 20-odd minutes. And at the end, a reporter from Connecticut asked her, very innocently, "Do you know you are compared to the American actress Brooke Shields?" At that point one of those goons in the blue GDR jackets leaned over and whispered in her ear, and she started speaking German.

Now, let's go to the 1987 World Championship in Cincinnati, which I still contend was the greatest that she ever skated and one of the three greatest per-formances I've ever seen. She's on the home turf of Debi Thomas, who is the reigning World champion. One day after practice, Jutta Muller sends Katarina into the stands to sign autographs for half an hour, in one of the great psycho-logical ploys of all time.

First of all, it reflected the East Germans' changed attitude about dealing with the outside world. And second, she won over the entire crowd in Cincinnati. And Alex McGowan [Thomas's coach] was furious. In the competition, Debi went out there with a bad foot and skated lights out, then Katarina went out there and skated even more lights out to beat her.

Everyone remembers the next year in Calgary—Katarina standing by the boards, staring Debi down. What I remember more than anything else was, again, the change in the East Germans through the two press conferences she had. The one beforehand, when she walked into the room and saw that auditorium with people hanging off the rafters and said, "Oh, my God!" Despite all the letters she'd received, despite everything, I think that was the first moment at which she became totally aware of the impact that she had on the West. Then after she won, she had to have several beers in order to supply a sample for the drug test, and during that press conference she was just giggling. It was pretty amusing.

Now, let's take this a couple of years down the line. We were having dinner in 1990, after the Wall had fallen. One of the British tabloids had done a story saying that she, like other East German athletes, was on steroids. I asked her about it, and in a way that only Katarina could, she leaned over the table and said, "Look at these boobs! If I were on steroids, would I have boobs like this?"

By the time she got to Albertville in 1992 and was doing stuff on the air for CBS, I remember how impressed I was. This was a girl who at one point had been the pinup girl of the president of the East German Republic, who obviously realized her position in that society and realized that if she played the way they wanted her to play the game, then she could have a better life. So for all of her life, she played by the rules that said white was black. Then, on October 3, 1989, black became white, the Wall fell and she was all of a sudden a pariah, looked upon by a lot of people in East Germany as someone who had taken advantage of things, while they were left with no money whatsoever.

And I was always extraordinarily impressed by the way that she handled that transition. She obviously was aware of things. She said, "It always used to strike me how unbelievable it was that those guards at the border gate couldn't move 10 feet, and I had just come back from the West." But I don't think she was truly aware of the depth of despair in her own country, and how that depth of despair led many people to see her not as a sports hero but as a flunky for the system, a system in which she played along, realizing that was in her and her family's best interests to do that. Yet she made the transition so smoothly, despite total dislocation in her life. It literally was going from white was black to black was white.

She was a ruthless competitor, ruthless in the best sense of the word. In Calgary she did all she had to do to win, and the rest of the time just flirted. But the year before in Cincinnati, she landed four and three-quarters triple jumps—five triple jumps back then were a lot. It was as though she was saying, "Have I proved to you I'm enough of an athlete now?"

Watching her go from this 18-year-old sex goddess from this gray country, to winning two Olympic titles, to becoming a well-paid, popular skater in the West, was one of the most interesting threads I've ever followed in figure skating.

FRANK ORR
Advance Notice

Sometimes the truth needs a little help working its way onto the printed page. In an earlier era of figure skating, there was no live television coverage and the World Championships didn't draw nearly the attention from the press that they do today. But then, as now, it was necessary for sportswriters to get the story from the horse's mouth. Readers wanted to hear from the athletes themselves, even if the quotes weren't as revealing as we've come to expect from 1990s news stories. It was up to the writer to get the words, no matter how it was done.

Until he had a serious heart attack in May of 1996, Frank Orr of the Toronto Star *had covered every Worlds since 1987, except the 1996 event in Lausanne, when a department decision altered his plans at the eleventh hour. But back in 1965 he was a first-time substitute for the regular figure skating writer, Jim Proudfoot, who had a scheduling conflict during the World Championships.*

Orr is Canada's king of the one-liners, and his off-the-cuff remarks are the stuff of legends in press boxes around the world. For example, during a particularly disastrous women's final at a Canadian Championship, when nearly every serious contender fell at least twice, Orr quipped, "Why don't they just send a picture of Barbara Ann Scott to the Worlds?"

Since Orr has an anecdote for every occasion, it's no surprise that he recalls an episode from the 1965 Worlds at Colorado Springs.

Out of eight journalists at the event, three of us were from Canada. It was a different time. Imagine a World Championships in the United States with eight accredited media! We didn't even have a press room. The Telex sent a man to the rink, and you'd write your story and he'd take it down to Western Union and send it for you. Now you'll have 300 accredited media. Still only three actually working, but 300 accredited.

For some reason, the head of the Canadian delegation decreed, after Petra Burka won her gold medal, that she should be given the chance to bask in her glory without being bothered by the media. We eventually beat this guy down and got maybe 90 seconds with Burka.

The next day, George Gross [of the old *Toronto Telegram*] and I were having breakfast with Donald Knight, who was skating that night. He'd just finished a practice, so he sat with us, which is something that wouldn't happen now— they'd never let an athlete near the media. Donald was pretty well slotted to finish third in Worlds, which he eventually did.

Anyway, Gross was quite aggravated by this official who had kept us from Burka and he mentioned it to Donald Knight, and Don said, "Well, guys, I'll save you the trouble."

He said, "I'll tell you what I'm going to say, right now."

He said, "If I finish third, this is why, and this is what I'll say."

He said, "If I luck into it, I know which one ahead of me will fail and I'll be able to move up one and this is what I'll say."

He said, "If I should really luck into the damn thing and win it, this is what I'll say as the World champion."

And he said, "Of course, if I screw it all up and I finish up the track, this is what I'll say about that."

So it was quite remarkable. You went to the event with the quotes from the guy you needed, before it ever started.

And ever since then, Don Knight has been one of my favorite athletes.

VERN LUNDQUIST

I Liked It, But Didn't Understand

*Vern Lundquist will be the voice of figure skating for CBS's coverage of the
Nagano Games, but this is a secondary contract. When Lundquist hired on he had
already left CBS for a better opportunity at Turner Broadcasting calling NFL
Sunday-night games, NBA basketball and all the network's figure skating properties.*

*In his TV broadcasting career, Lundquist has acquired an extensive portfolio
in football—he spent four years on air with ex-quarterback Terry Bradshaw on
CBS's NFL broadcasts—college basketball, college football, pro basketball and big-
time golf. He was a latecomer to skating—although he has made up for lost time.*

*When CBS landed the rights to the Albertville Olympics, Lundquist assumed
he'd be doing alpine events because he lives in Steamboat Springs, Colorado, and
was acquainted with some of America's top skiers. But CBS executive producer
Tim Shaker eschewed the obvious and decided to team him with Scott Hamilton
on figure skating. The broadcasting partnership became one of figure skating's
best and most recognizable, and grew into a strong friendship.*

Scott and I had met once at the 1981 National Sports Festival when he
was still competing and I was at ABC. Other than that, I didn't know him
except by reputation. We first worked together at the 1989 World Junior
Championships in Colorado Springs at the Broadmoor.

This is absolutely true—I'd never seen a figure skating event. Ever.

I walked into the building—that old World Arena at the Broadmoor,
[which] was kind of a ramshackle thing in its latter days—went to my left and
was standing in the corner behind the plexiglass. This guy on the ice comes
toward me, backward, and I said, "Now, that's kinda intriguing," and he got
maybe 15 feet away from me and executed what I later learned was a triple
Lutz. I didn't know what the hell was going on. Just that he's coming at me with
a whole lot of speed—backward!—and all of a sudden he puts his foot in the
ice and explodes straight up, turns around three times and skates out of my
field of vision.

It was Elvis Stojko.

The first guy I ever saw jump was Elvis. In light of subsequent events, it really took on enormous meaning for me that it was Stojko who was the first guy.

Jessica Mills had finished second in Junior Worlds the previous year, and Bob Mansbach, the producer of the event, whose lack of knowledge of figure skating was exceeded only by my own, said, "She's naturally going to be the Olympic favorite." We were all ready to anoint Jessica Mills as the next Olympic champion in 1992. She was going to be America's sweetheart. When Scott arrived he said, "Um, guys. No. She's not that good of an athlete...don't do this."

I watched her skate and I thought she skated very well. When it was over, she got fairly low marks. She had a pout on her face and I went over to her, and I remember saying, "That seemed like a pretty good performance to me." And she said, "Yes, except I doubled every triple jump." I knew the concept was to stand up and skate prettily. But I had no clue. And then when Yuka Sato skated and fell down two or three times and won, I thought, "This is really an unusual sport."

I liked what I saw, but I couldn't understand any of it.

The real tip-off for me came a month later at the Europeans. Scott and I had a chance to spend a lot of time together at that event. I remember walking into the arena with him the first day of practice. Here again, subsequent events have made this loom a lot larger for me than it probably was at the time. I saw Katia and Sergei warming up behind the boards and Scott introduced me to them. And then Mishkuteniok and Dmitriev were on the ice in a practice session, and I thought, "God, this is something!"

I'd been around television and sports all my adult life, and I'd been with the networks since 1984, so I'd dealt with a lot of the major players in sports. I was used to traveling through cities and airports and watching people come up to celebrities, and them interacting with people.

One of my most vivid memories is walking into that arena in Leningrad [now St. Petersburg] with Scott and watching him try to get from one side to the other. In my mind it took an hour, although it was probably more like 15 to 20 minutes. He signed every autograph, patted every head and said hello to everybody who said hello to him. [He was] just mobbed by friendly faces—welcomed would be the better word. They were so thrilled that he was in the building.

Watching him acknowledge the people who loved him and who loved the sport, and the grace with which he conducted himself, made an impression on me that I've never, ever forgotten.

BEVERLEY SMITH

Bev, You're Next

This is a tale of how flexible, both literally and figuratively, reporters must some-times be in getting the information required for the stories that will appear in the next day's paper.

Beverley Smith is Canada's most widely respected figure skating journalist and has been a fixture on the national and international scene for nearly two decades. She is a tireless interviewer, whose workday during a competition regu-larly exceeds 16 hours, all spent either rinkside or huddled over her laptop as she races toward the Globe and Mail's *several deadlines.*

She has written several influential books on figure skating, and her debut work, Figure Skating: A Celebration, *was an international bestseller in 1995, creating a slipstream for dozens of skating books by other authors.*

Despite the following anecdote, we can testify that Beverley Smith is a diligent and energetic figure skating writer and a good friend, not a "basket case."

I was supposed to be taking part in a Michelle Kwan conference call a few days before the 1997 Champions Series Final. It was to be at 2:15 P.M., but Michelle got her time zones mixed up, with the three hours difference on the West Coast, so it ended up scheduled for 5:15.

The juggling caused me a lot of problems, because not only was it right against my deadline, but I had already scheduled a massage therapist to come into my house to work on my back—my muscles were all knotted up from having written 97,000 words on the book I had just completed.

So at the last minute everything changed. I thought everything was still going to be okay, because the appointment was from four to five, and the ther-apist would be finished just in time for me to take part in the conference call.

But the therapist got lost on the way to my house. I was pacing up and down, wondering what I was going to do. She didn't show up until 20 min-utes before the call was supposed to start and her sessions are an hour long. I couldn't make her wait until I finished this conference call because she had other things on her schedule. And I couldn't *not* do [the call], because I was going away to the competition the next day. And I also really wanted to hear what Michelle Kwan had to say. It would really be the first time she talked since she'd lost Nationals, and she'd had some time to think about it.

We went ahead with the massage session, and I was lying on a table under the sheet, with my head in a basket at the end of the table, so I was in no position to have a phone in my ear. So I made a deal with my therapist that when the phone rang, she would pick it up, and when the operator said, "Is this Beverley Smith?" she would just say yes to avoid confusion. I'd then turn on my tape recorder, which was attached to the phone. And that's exactly what happened. I couldn't hear the press conference because I was about four feet from the phone.

What I didn't know until later was that the conversation came around to people wondering what Michelle weighed. Christine Brennan [sportswriter], who was in on the conference, volunteered to say how tall she herself was and how much she weighed. And then she said, "Bev, you're next," thinking I was on the line because I'd been announced at the start of the call. And, of course, I was not. She probably figured I was extremely insulted at being asked to reveal my weight... there was a long silence before anyone said anything.

But I wasn't actually on the phone—I had my head in a basket.

JIM PROUDFOOT

Play It Again, Jim

Jim Proudfoot is one of the true gentlemen in the world of Canadian sportswriting. No one in North America has been covering the sport as consistently, or for as long, as Proudfoot has for the Toronto Star. *He was among the first newsmen to treat figure skating as a mainstream sport, sometimes over the objection of narrow-minded colleagues.*

Proudfoot has known the Jelinek family since 1955, when the brother-sister team of Otto and Maria won the national junior pairs title in Toronto. The Jelineks had been a wealthy and influential family in Prague prior to the postwar Communist takeover of Czechoslovakia, and the story of their harrowing 1948 escape from that regime was well told in the book On Thin Ice.

When the World Championships were held in Prague in 1962, a series of political maneuvers had supposedly guaranteed the safety of the returning expatriate Jelinek siblings, but their parents could not be completely sure. Proudfoot was asked by Henry and Jarmila Jelinek—who could not return to their native country—to watch over their children, which he did. Otto and Maria won the gold medal over a rising Soviet pair, the Protopopovs, and Proudfoot's friendship with the family was solidified.

Proudfoot calls his relationship with "old Henry Jelinek and his wife a special experience. This was an Old World aristocrat with all the manners and culture of old Europe. Something you might see in motion pictures. He really was a character in the best sense of the word.

"Our job does bring us into contact with great people."

I was at the 1977 World Hockey championship—the first in which NHL players participated—in Vienna, and Henry Jelinek was there was his wife, Jarmila. They always took a spring holiday in Europe, preferably in Vienna, where they would be installed in a magnificent suite in the Imperial Hotel. Of course, those were the Iron Curtain days, and some of their old friends from Czechoslovakia would come over to Vienna to visit, because the Jelineks could not go back into Czechoslovakia.

We'd been in touch, but I, of course, was very busy during the championships, and he asked if I could stay in Vienna a few days so we'd have a chance to visit. But I was scheduled to go home when the tournament ended, and I said something like, "There is only one thing that would keep me here, and that is, on Thursday night—this was a Sunday—there is an anniversary presentation at the Vienna Opera House." The conductor, Herbert von Karajan, was coming back from Germany to conduct these two or three performances. The opera was *Il Trovatore*, with Pavarotti as the star tenor. I said, "If I thought I could get a ticket to *that*, I'd stay," but it would be ridiculous to think of that—it had been sold out for months. The Vienna Opera House isn't that big to start with and this was one of the great operatic events in the history of the art form—I said, "I'm gone." He said, "I don't see any problem getting tickets."

So he did get the tickets and I did stay. I always think of it as one of the great evenings of my life. I love to recount it.

I went to their suite and had a drink to begin the evening. There was a car to drive us over to the opera house. It would have been a nice stroll, but not as swanky. We had nice seats, and unlike most places where one would attend an opera, [the audience] was very knowledgeable and excitable. First of all they went crazy over the conductor, who had left Vienna for Berlin, then over the arias sung by Pavarotti. You'd have thought the audience would never stop cheering—like no hockey game you ever saw.

The next thing was supper in the famous Red Bar of the Sacher Hotel, where the dessert Sacher torte was invented 300 years ago. The piano player jumped up and clicked his heels: "Good evening, Herr Jelinek." He came over and asked what tunes we'd like played, and Henry said we'd like to hear a medley from *Il Trovatore*. We had a nice supper and it was all over by midnight.

Toward the end of his life, after his wife died, old Henry Jelinek was still the same vibrant character, but his frontiers were shrunken by sheer age. His eyesight failed and then deserted him completely. He continued to live in their gorgeous condo alone after his wife died, and I visited him as often as I could, although not as often as I would have liked.

And he always loved to hear me recount the story of our great evening. He'd sort of prompt me, "What was that time in Vienna, Jim? Jarmila was there, wasn't she?" And pretty soon I'd see he'd want me to retell the whole thing.

He'd particularly like the part about the piano player jumping up and clicking his heels in the fabulous, legendary Red Bar of the Sacher Hotel.

He was blind, so he'd just sit there with a sort of beatific expression on his face, as if he was reveling in the memory just as much as I was.

CHRISTINE BRENNAN

Overreaction

A surge in popularity is always a double-edged (at least) sword. As your newly discovered assets are held up for widespread public scrutiny, so are your liabilities. Thus it was only a matter of time before all the attention on figure skating would create situations that seemed uncomfortable to some who'd spent a lifetime in the sport. It can be easily argued that the very linchpin of skating's explosion in popularity—the Harding–Kerrigan incident—was one such awkward occasion.

Another was the USFSA's 1996 attempt to ban the well-respected Washington Post *reporter Christine Brennan from covering official events. After her groundbreaking book,* Inside Edge, *appeared earlier that year, the USFSA, through its president, Morry Stillwell, and its executive director, Jerry Lace, notified the* Post *that Brennan would no longer be afforded "media services normally offered" to*

reporters at USFSA events. "It is our opinion that Ms. Brennan no longer is report-
ing figure skating on an impartial basis and has interjected her personal opinions
into her coverage of the sport, whether it be for additional sales of her book or her
notion that she is the protector of the sport of figure skating," they wrote.

Brennan, who holds a master's degree from Northwestern University, first
started covering figure skating at the 1988 Olympics. She and Phil Hersh have
become the unofficial leaders of the U.S. skating press corps. Despite leaving the
newspaper in late 1996 to concentrate more on writing books—the success of
Inside Edge *gave her the financial freedom to do so—she still freelances skating*
articles to the Post. *It is one of the world's most highly regarded papers, a paper*
that has the reputation of going to the wall for its writers, as underscored by the
fallout surrounding its exposure of the Watergate affair.

When I got my promotional copies of the book, I sent one out as a courtesy to the USFSA a full month before the publication date. They knew all about it. They knew that I was working on it. Let them see it. "If you've got any problems, give me a call. We're going to have a two-way street." I never hear a word.

In January, we're at the U.S. nationals at San Jose. I see them—them being [USFSA executive director] Jerry Lace and [USFSA president] Morry Stillwell. Everything's fine.

February. Nothing. I don't see them. Everything's fine.

March. Worlds in Edmonton. Jerry Lace comes up and gives me a big hug. Jerry's that kind of guy—he's very open and wants to be friendly. Nothing said.

Early April, the same day Greg Norman fell apart at the Masters, a Sunday, I'm at the *Post* working on a story about an Olympic sailor, and I go to my mailbox and there's a letter from the United States Figure Skating Association. I open it up, figuring it's a press release or something, and it's a c.c. copy of a letter to my boss, George Solomon. Basically, it says that the USFSA will not give Christine Brennan credentials anymore. The *Washington Post* can send anyone else, but not Christine Brennan.

I looked at this letter and I thought it was an April Fools' joke. I was stunned. I read it again and I realized it wasn't a joke and they were serious. My first reaction was consternation, concern—"This is kind of funny, but it really isn't funny." What have I done? What's going on?

Monday, George Soloman calls up [the USFSA]. "Yes, indeed, we're banning Christine Brennan," says Jerry Lace. Then a six-week negotiation process begins.

A couple of things important to know. I never, ever got involved in any phone calls. I moved away from that. The *Washington Post* does such a nice job at those kinds of things. They've been through this with bigger organizations than the USFSA...the White House comes to mind. Within a week or two it's pretty clear the USFSA is going to rescind [the ban]. Relent. Back down. But exactly how it's going to work, so that they can save face, is yet to be determined. Another thing to keep in mind is that there was a threatened boycott of USFSA events by APSE, the Associated Press Sports Editors, representing over 300 papers in the U.S.

So the reaction was terrific. I have to say that after those first moments of being worried, within 24 hours it was so clear that the support was so strong that I felt that this was going to work out just fine. So throughout most of the rest of it I kept a sense of humor. One of the first messages I received was a fax from Dick Button. And he wrote, "Christine, you naughty, naughty, naughty, naughty, naughty, naughty girl, you. Congratulations." When you get something like that you say to yourself, "All right, I can handle this. I'm going to have a sense of humor here. This isn't life and death. We're going to win this thing and all will be well."

And it was. By the end of May, they had relented. I had the credentials back. There was no problem with Skate America. And I've been to credentialed events since then. My personal relations? Pretty good. Jerry Lace comes up and shakes my hand and goes, "Uhhhh, remind me of your name again?" and we laugh. Morry Stillwell—that friendship I don't think is ever going to happen again. I'm not even sure if [the problem] was the book. I kind of think it is something a little bit different.

On a book tour, you talk about the book, you talk about the sport. You're seen. You're on TV. Radio. In newspapers. You can almost get sick of yourself. You're sick of what you're saying. It's almost like a presidential candidate— you're hearing the same thing over and over again.

I don't know this for a fact, but I'm wondering if they got sick of seeing me. I'm not sure—this is just a guess—that perhaps they said to themselves, "We've had just about enough out of her. She's not a skater. She never was a skater. She's not one of ours. How dare she talk about our sport?"

I think figure skating is exploding in front of our eyes. You've got a sport with the professional, "ineligible," side and the Olympic, "eligible," side. There's confusion. You and I could get a sponsor and a network and put on a competition. There's no Good Housekeeping Seal of Approval. There's no commissioner. There's no nothing. It's the Wild West.

As it's exploding in interest, of course the media will tend to come and see what's going on. I think over the years that the figure skating establishment has come to believe that a commentator saying, "Oh, what a lovely jump!" is journalism. As we know, that's not journalism. Real journalists, like the bunch who are now around the sport, start asking questions and start raising serious issues. While we talk about the lovely jumps, we also talk about AIDS. And while we talk about the beautiful performances, we also talk about the fact that they're very young girls...being tutored—they're not in school. Raising questions, not answering them, just bringing up issues. I don't think they like that.

I think the establishment of the sport would rather that those issues not be raised. Well, when you have the second most popular television sport in the United States, only behind the National Football League, those questions not only should be raised, they have to be raised.

And I'm very proud to raise them.

CAM COLE

The Beauty and Brutality

It validates figure skating when a heavy hitter like Cam Cole, who made his name and his journalistic style in mainstream sports, drops into the sport out of necessity and stays with it out of interest. This is a far more common occurrence in Canada, with people like Cole, his arch rival and friend, Terry Jones, and Toronto's Jim Proudfoot. In the United States, famous columnists and beat writers from pro sports tend to parachute in to apply their touch to the megastories—the Tonya–Nancy extreme, the Olympic Games, the little-girl syndrome—but somehow can't, or don't want to, grasp the sustaining essence of the sport. They usually leave carrying the same attitude toward figure skating that they arrived with.

Cole, the star of the Edmonton Journal *and principal national sports columnist for Southam, Canada's dominant newspaper empire, was forced into figure skating when the Royal Glenora Club in Edmonton became an international power in the mid-1980s. The Glenora, still a force, was then home to the likes of Kurt Browning and Kristi Yamaguchi.*

Cole, a penetrating observer, is sensitive to the unique qualities of skating, but brings to the sport an objectivity honed in covering football, hockey, boxing and golf.

I approached the sport sort of on tiptoes. I didn't really know what to think of having to go down to the rink and talk to figure skaters. I'd never been into figure skating as a kid, never enjoyed it. The closest I'd ever been to it was sort of watching some women figure skate after hockey practice when I was a kid.

I met Browning for the first time and thought, "Now, here is kind of a neat kid." You know Kurt—he's got lots of style and lots of charm and a good sense of humor. I think it was probably Kurt Browning's quotes—just the way he conveyed ideas—that drew me near enough to the sport to look at it with open eyes. I think I could appreciate, finally, by watching Kurt and hearing him talk about the sport that this was an athletic event, that this wasn't a ballet contest. This was for athletes.

The nearer I got—as a commentator, or whatever you call it—the more I began to respect the brutality of the sport, if you can put it that way.

One of the first things I covered in my career was boxing. And to me figure skating is very comparable to boxing. It is very much the same loneliness when you step on the stage. If anything, the people in this sport have to be mentally tougher. And to me, there is nothing, *nothing*, in sports that I've ever experienced that can compare to the lonely feeling I get, the feeling of empathy [I have] for the loneliness that athlete has, standing out there in the middle of the ice, waiting for the music to start, when everything's on the line. I went through it a number of times with Browning. I've gone through it a number of times now with Stojko. And every single time that those guys stand out there and do the job, I'm in awe of them.

I can think of three or four or five times in other sports, in a 20-some-year writing career, that I've ever gotten to the climax of an event and found a little tear in the corner of my eye—Jack Nicklaus winning the Masters in 1986, the Oilers winning their first Stanley Cup at home with all those great young players who had kind of grown up together. But when I watched Browning skate to those World titles and watch Stojko skate to the World titles, every time, I'm sitting there wiping a little tear away from the corner of my eye and saying, "This is one of the greatest things in sport that I'll ever see in my lifetime."

The first time that I can ever recall being struck by the powerful emotion that this sport drives was in the press box at the 1988 Olympics when Midori

Ito was skating. Midori at that time was, within the skating community, known somewhat, but it was still a major surprise, I think, for her do those superb performances in Calgary and light up the place with that smile.

There were guys there I had covered hockey with, sports columnists, guys from the southern United States, football guys, NASCAR guys, guys who basically were approaching this thing in a pretty skeptical manner. And I saw a whole lot of those guys up there, when she finished her performance that night, taking their glasses off and wiping their eyes with their hands.

And I'm thinking to myself, "Now you know...now you know."